Table of Contents

W9-BRM-645

Introduction

What Is Readers' Theater?

One good way to gain an understanding of readers' theater is to first get a clear picture of what it is *not*. Readers' theater is not a fully-staged production with sets, costumes, and dramatic action performed by actors who memorize lines from a script. Instead, a readers' theater performance is a dramatic reading, just as its name suggests. Readers are usually seated, reading from a script that is held in their hands or placed on a music stand in front of them. There may be minimal use of costumes or props, such as hats, a scepter or crown, or a simple backdrop to provide a suggestion of the setting and characters that the readers hope to bring to life for the audience during their dramatic reading.

Readers' theater offers all the enrichment of traditional theater productions, but without the logistical challenges that come with designing and building sets and creating costumes. Students are spared the stress of having to memorize lines, and can instead focus on developing a strong dramatic reading of the script.

How to Integrate *Readers' Theater* into Your Classroom

The *Readers' Theater* scripts may be used in a variety of settings for a range of educational purposes. Consider the following:

Language Arts blocks are ideal for incorporating *Readers' Theater* scripts, with their emphasis on reading aloud with expression. Many of the follow-up activities that accompany each script address key skills from the reading/language arts curriculum.

Content-Area Instruction can come alive when you use a *Readers' Theater* script to help explore social studies, science, or math concepts. Check the Table of Contents for the grade-level content-area connections in each script.

Integrated Thematic Teaching can continue throughout the day when you use *Readers' Theater* scripts to help you maintain your thematic focus across all areas of the curriculum, from language arts instruction through content-area lessons.

School Assemblies and Holiday Programs provide the perfect opportunity to showcase student performances. Consider presenting a *Readers' Theater* performance for Black History Month, Women's History Month, for parent evenings, or any other occasion when your students are invited to perform.

Teaching the *Readers' Theater* Units

The 15 units in this volume each include the following:

- A **teacher page** to help you plan instruction:

A short **summary** gives you an overview of each script's plot.

Use the **number of parts** to choose the number of readers to assign per role. Or, you may wish to create two or more casts for each production.

Background information provides facts that you may need to know about the subject treated in the script. It also guides you in activating students' prior knowledge or in building background about new or unfamiliar topics. This helps promote success for students as they approach each new script.

A **unit-level table of contents** gives you at-a-glance information on the script and the follow-up activities.

Vocabulary that may be new or unfamiliar to students is called out so that you can introduce it prior to reading the script.

Staging ideas may be included for some scripts. These optional ideas offer quick and easy suggestions to help both readers and their audience connect with the characters and setting of the play.

An **encore** feature for some scripts includes quick, optional ideas to extend learning related to the content of the script. Ideas range from retelling activities and related literature to ideas for other types of performances.

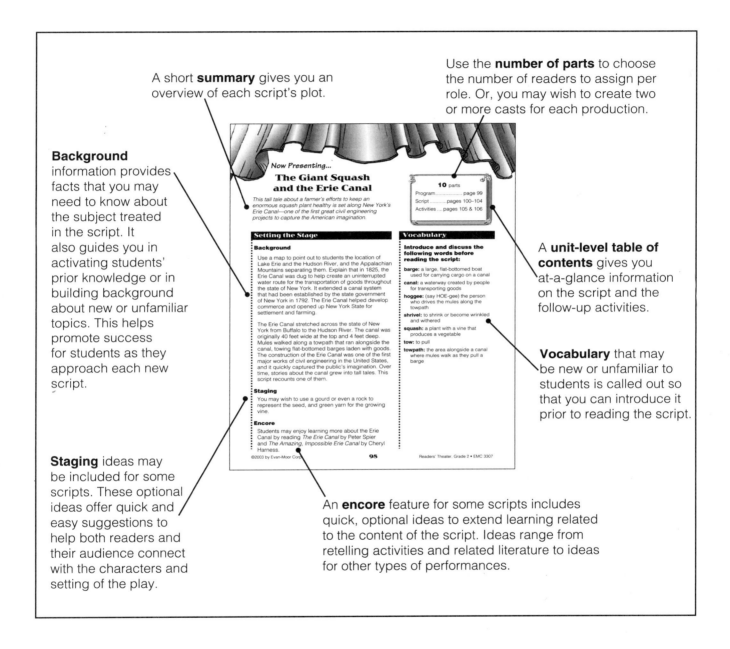

Now Presenting...

The Giant Squash and the Erie Canal

This tall tale about a farmer's efforts to keep an enormous squash plant healthy is set along New York's Erie Canal—one of the first great civil engineering projects to capture the American imagination.

10 parts

Program..................page 99
Script ....pages 100–104
Activities ....pages 105 & 106

Setting the Stage

Background

Use a map to point out to students the location of Lake Erie and the Hudson River, and the Appalachian Mountains separating them. Explain that in 1825, the Erie Canal was dug to help create an uninterrupted water route for the transportation of goods throughout the state of New York. It extended a canal system that had been established by the state government of New York in 1792. The Erie Canal helped develop commerce and opened up New York State for settlement and farming.

The Erie Canal stretched across the state of New York from Buffalo to the Hudson River. The canal was originally 40 feet wide at the top and 4 feet deep. Mules walked along a towpath that ran alongside the canal, towing flat-bottomed barges laden with goods. The construction of the Erie Canal was one of the first major works of civil engineering in the United States, and it quickly captured the public's imagination. Over time, stories about the canal grew into tall tales. This script recounts one of them.

Staging

You may wish to use a gourd or even a rock to represent the seed, and green yarn for the growing vine.

Encore

Students may enjoy learning more about the Erie Canal by reading *The Erie Canal* by Peter Spier and *The Amazing, Impossible Erie Canal* by Cheryl Harness.

©2003 by Evan-Moor Corp.

98

Vocabulary

Introduce and discuss the following words before reading the script:

barge: a large, flat-bottomed boat used for carrying cargo on a canal

canal: a waterway created by people for transporting goods

hoggee: (say HOE-gee) the person who drives the mules along the towpath

shrivel: to shrink or become wrinkled and withered

squash: a plant with a vine that produces a vegetable

tow: to pull

towpath: the area alongside a canal where mules walk as they pull a barge

Readers' Theater, Grade 2 • EMC 3307

- A reproducible **program** page provides an introduction to the script and a list of characters. Use this page to list the names of students who will read each role, and distribute it to your audience to enhance the theater-going experience.

- The **script** is the heart of the *Readers' Theater* volume. This is the reproducible four- or five-page text that students will read during rehearsals and performances. You may wish to read the script aloud to students before assigning parts and beginning rehearsal readings. Once you have read through the script as a group, you may wish to assign students to work independently in small groups while you interact with other student groups.

- Two or three pages of follow-up **activities** may be assigned once students have completed a first reading of the script. Activities are designed to be completed independently, and may be conducted while you provide individualized or small-group instruction or hold a rehearsal with another group of students.

Meeting Individual Needs

Struggling readers may be partnered with one or more stronger readers who all read the same role together. This group support is often enough to allow struggling readers to participate fully in the activity. Struggling readers may also be able to independently read parts that have a repeating refrain or a simple rhyme pattern.

Students acquiring English may benefit from using the same approaches as for struggling readers. In addition, you may wish to create an audio recording of the script to provide English learners the opportunity to listen to fluent English pronunciation of the script as they follow along with the written text.

Accelerated learners may be challenged to transform *Readers' Theater* scripts into fully-staged productions by adding stage directions, planning props and sets, and even developing or expanding the existing dialog. You might also use such students as "directors," helping to manage small-group rehearsals for class *Readers' Theater* productions.

Evaluating Student Performance

Use the templates provided on pages 5 and 6 to help students plan and evaluate their performances. You may copy and distribute the templates just as they are, or use them to guide you in leading a class discussion about the criteria for evaluating *Readers' Theater* performances. Students may also develop their own iconography (e.g., one or two thumbs up, thumbs down, 1 to 5 stars, etc.) to rate their own performances and those of their classmates. Encourage students to be thoughtful in providing feedback, stressing the importance of sharing ways to improve, as well as highlighting successful aspects of the performance. You may wish to conduct performance reviews during the rehearsal stage in order to give students an opportunity to incorporate suggestions for improvement. You may also wish to compare those comments to feedback following the final performance. Use the template on page 7 to conduct your own assessment of students' acquisition of language arts skills during *Readers' Theater* activities.

Pre-performance Checklist

Name _____

1. Did you listen to a reading of the script?
   ☐ **Yes**
   ☐ **No** – Ask your teacher, another adult, or a classmate to read it to you.

2. Did you highlight all your lines in the script?
   ☐ **Yes**
   ☐ **No** – Use a highlighting pen to go over all your lines.

3. Did you mark places where you must pause between lines?
   ☐ **Yes**
   ☐ **No** – Use a mark like this: / /

4. Have you collected any materials or props that you will use?
   ☐ **Yes**
   ☐ **No** – Ask your teacher or other cast members for ideas if you need help.

5. Have you chosen and practiced any movements, faces, or speaking styles you will use?
   ☐ **Yes**
   ☐ **No** – Ask your teacher or other cast members for ideas if you need help.

6. Have you practiced reading your lines with expression?
   ☐ **Yes**
   ☐ **No** – Try out your ideas with a partner or another cast member.

7. Have you participated in a rehearsal and gotten performance feedback?
   ☐ **Yes**
   ☐ **No** – Have a reviewer focus on your participation in the play. After you get feedback, find ways to make changes to improve your performance.

Performance Review Template

Date: _____   Title of play: _____

☐ Rehearsal
☐ Performance

1. I am reviewing
   ☐ one reader   Name: _____   Role: _____
   ☐ the entire performance

2. I could see the reader(s).
   ☐ Yes
   ☐ Needs improvement   Name(s): _____

3. I could hear the reader(s).
   ☐ Yes
   ☐ Needs to speak more loudly   Name(s): _____

4. I could understand the reader(s).
   ☐ Yes
   ☐ Needs to speak more clearly   Name(s): _____

5. The reader(s) used good expression.
   ☐ Yes
   ☐ Needs to improve   Name(s): _____

6. The use of gestures was
   ☐ just right
   ☐ not enough; use more
   ☐ too much; use fewer   Name(s): _____

Other comments:

_____

_____

_____

_____

Assessing Oral Presentations

As you observe students during rehearsals or performances, focus on the following areas in assessing individual students.

Date: _____

Title of play: _____

☐ Rehearsal

☐ Performance

Name: _____   Role: _____

1. Student speaks clearly.	☐ Yes	☐ Needs improvement
2. Student speaks at appropriate pace.	☐ Yes	☐ Needs improvement
3. Student speaks fluently, using appropriate intonation, expression, and emphasis.	☐ Yes	☐ Needs improvement
4. Student enlivens reading with gestures and facial expressions.	☐ Yes	☐ Needs improvement
5. Student prepared and used appropriate props.	☐ Yes	☐ Not applicable
6. Student participated actively in rehearsals.	☐ Yes	☐ Needs improvement
7. Student contributed appropriately to this production.	☐ Yes	☐ Needs improvement

Other comments: _____

_____

_____

_____

Now Presenting...

John Chapman

John Chapman was an unusual person. Popularly known as Johnny Appleseed, he changed our world by planting apple trees throughout the Midwest.

Setting the Stage

Background

Make sure students know that legends often grow out of stories about people who really lived. This is the case with John Chapman, who was born in 1774 and later came to be known as Johnny Appleseed. He traveled throughout six states, planting apple seeds and seedlings as he went in an effort to fulfill his dream of spreading apple orchards throughout the land. Because of his strange dress, vegetarian eating habits, and his unusual dream, people began telling stories about the events in his life. This script is an imaginary episode in the life of an extraordinary man who believed that all people and animals were his friends.

Staging

Have the person reading John Chapman's part wear a pan on his head.

Vocabulary

Review with students the meaning of these terms related to apple farming:

blossom: the flower or bloom of a fruit-bearing plant or tree

nursery: a place where young trees or plants are raised

seedling: a plant grown from a seed

Use a map of the United States to point out the states where John Chapman planted apple trees. Help students learn to read and pronounce these state names:

Illinois

Indiana

Kentucky

Massachusetts

Ohio

Pennsylvania

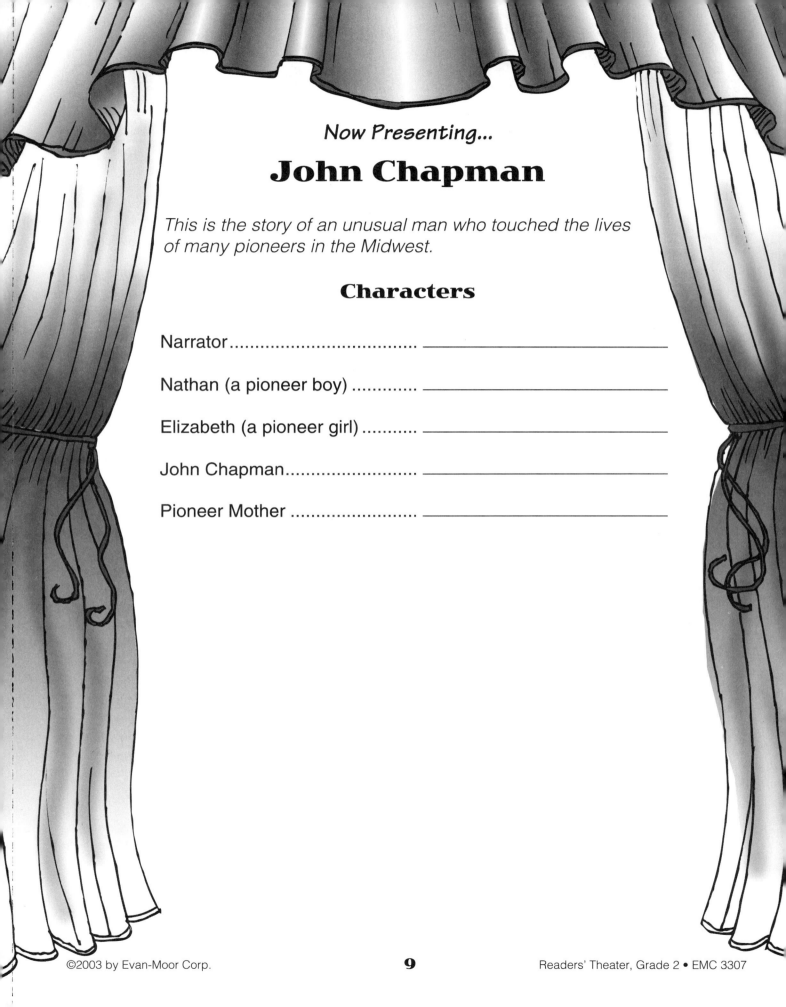

Now Presenting...

John Chapman

This is the story of an unusual man who touched the lives of many pioneers in the Midwest.

Characters

Narrator .... _____

Nathan (a pioneer boy) .... _____

Elizabeth (a pioneer girl) .... _____

John Chapman.......................... _____

Pioneer Mother .... _____

John Chapman

···················· **Characters** ····················

Narrator	John Chapman
Nathan	Pioneer Mother
Elizabeth	

Narrator: John Chapman was born in Leominster, Massachusetts, in the year 1774. He grew up to become a very special man. His dream was to plant apple trees all over the Midwest. He wanted pioneers to have apple trees for food when they settled the new lands. Let us take up our story in the year 1802. John Chapman, now 28 years old, is busy planting apple seedlings in the state of Ohio.

Elizabeth: *(excitedly; out of breath)* Nathan! Nathan! Come with me! I just saw the strangest thing!

Nathan: What is it?

Elizabeth: It's a man with a pan on his head! He's down by the river.

Narrator: The children run down to the river to find the man.

Elizabeth: Look! There he is!

Nathan: Hello, sir. I am Nathan Smith. My family is moving west to Illinois. Our wagons are right over that hill.

John: Hello, Nathan. My name is John Chapman, but most people call me Johnny Appleseed.

Nathan: Why do they call you that?

John: Because I spend so much time planting apple trees.

Elizabeth: Do you live here?

John: No, I'm just here planting apple trees. I want people to have apples for food when they build their homes here. As soon as I plant these last trees, I will be on my way.

Elizabeth: *(giggling)* Why are you wearing a pan on your head?

John: This is my cooking pan, and it fits just right.

Elizabeth: Did you lose your shoes in the river?

John: I don't much like shoes. Mostly, I like to go barefoot.

Nathan: May we help you plant these seedlings?

John: That would be wonderful. Let me show you how.

Elizabeth: Mama says we'll have to plant our own apple trees when we reach Illinois. It will be good to learn now how to do it. We will have to plant 50 trees on our new farm. That's what the law says.

John: Then it's a good thing that we've met here today! I hope some day to see apple blossoms all across this land. I have several nurseries where I raise these little apple trees. That is where these seedlings came from.

Nathan: *(out of breath)* It's mighty hard work digging this hole!

Elizabeth: But it would be easy work to eat an apple pie made from the apples that will grow on this tree.

Nathan: You sure must like apples a lot, Mr. Chapman.

John: I surely do! And I like berries and roots, too. That's what I eat most of the time. I live off the land. And this glorious land certainly does offer me plenty!

Elizabeth: And there will be even more by the time you finish planting these trees! People will certainly be thankful to you.

Mother: *(yelling)* Nathan! Elizabeth! Where are you?

Nathan: We're over here, Mama. We're learning to plant apple trees.

Mother: So I see . . . You must be the man we've been hearing about everywhere we go. Are you the gentleman who plants apple trees all over the countryside?

John: Few people have called me a gentleman, ma'am. Most people just call me Johnny Appleseed. And I guess I've just about finished up my work here. Why don't you take these last seedlings to plant at your new home? And perhaps we'll meet once again in Illinois. I'm headed that way.

Elizabeth and Nathan: Good-bye, Johnny Appleseed! Thank you! Until we meet again in Illinois!

Narrator: And so John Chapman moved on westward, planting apple trees and seeds as he went. He planted apple orchards in Pennsylvania, Ohio, Kentucky, Illinois, and Indiana. He also started many apple tree nurseries. He was a man with a wonderful dream, and he worked hard to make it come true!

John Chapman Travels West

John Chapman planted thousands of apple seeds and seedlings. The script lists the six states where he planted apple orchards.

- Find the states where John Chapman planted apple trees. Color these states red.
- Find the state where you live. Color it green.
- Make a blue dot in the state where you were born.
- Color the states you have visited purple.

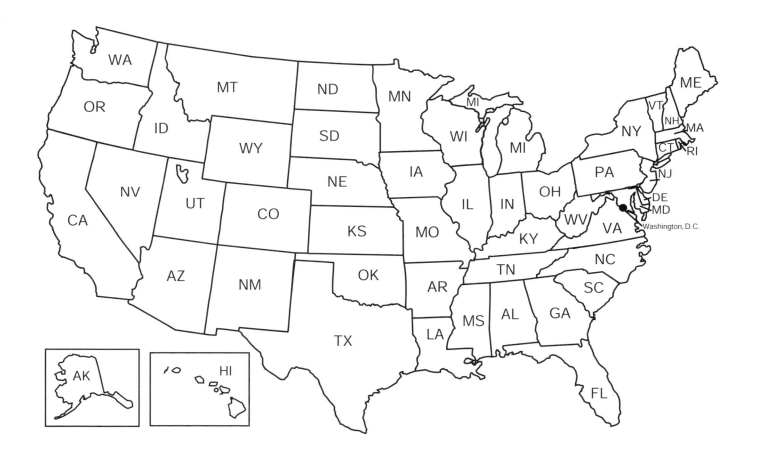

Name _____

U.S. Postage Stamp

A 5¢ U.S. postage stamp was recently issued to honor the memory of John Chapman. Design your own postage stamp in honor of Johnny Appleseed, the man who dreamed of apple blossoms all across America.

Johnny Appleseed

Word Box

apple

pie

berries

roots

blossoms

seedling

pan

shoes

Across

2. John Chapman liked to eat _____.
3. He also liked to eat _____.
7. A young, small apple tree is called a _____.

Down

1. Elizabeth liked to eat apple _____.
2. John Chapman wanted to see apple _____ all across the land.
4. John Chapman did not like to wear _____.
5. John Chapman spent most of his time planting _____ seeds.
6. Sometimes John Chapman wore a _____ on his head.

Now Presenting...

Crow's Potlatch

In this story from the Salish people of the Pacific Northwest, Lazy Raven is looking for someone to trick. He has not gathered food for the winter and is very hungry. Poor Crow learns a hard lesson about vanity.

Setting the Stage

Background

You may need to explain to students that a potlatch is a traditional form of celebration among the Native American peoples of the northwest coast of North America. Potlatches include singing, storytelling, dancing, and lots of food. A potlatch may be held by a family to honor births, deaths, marriages, the raising of totem poles, or the dedication of a house. The word *potlatch* comes from the Nootka word *p'achitl*, which means "to give a gift."

Encourage students to share what they know about ravens and crows. Be sure they know that ravens are larger than crows—about the size of a hawk—while crows are similar to pigeons in size. Ravens also have slightly heavier bills and more fan-shaped tails. Ravens sometimes have a ruff of feathers around their throat, and have a lower, more croaking call than crows.

Staging

Students may create and wear animal headbands depicting their characters during the reading.

Vocabulary

Introduce and discuss the following words before reading the script:

beware: be on guard; be careful

clever: bright; intelligent

hibernate: to spend the winter in sleep

hoarse: having a rough voice

store: to put something away to use later

trudge: a tired or heavy walk

vain: having too much pride in the way you look or act

Now Presenting...

Crow's Potlatch

This Native American story from the Pacific Northwest tells of Raven—a lazy, tricky bird. Just listen to the way he fools Crow into giving him food for the winter!

Characters

Narrator .... _____

Chorus .... _____

_____

_____

Crow .... _____

Raven .... _____

Squirrel .... _____

Deer .... _____

Rabbit .... _____

Readers' Theater, Grade 2 • EMC 3307

Crow's Potlatch

···················· **Characters** ····················

Narrator   Squirrel
Chorus   Deer
Crow   Rabbit
Raven

Narrator: We welcome you to our reading of "Crow's Potlatch." Potlatch is a Native American custom in the Pacific Northwest. It is a grand celebration. There is singing, dancing, and lots of food. Listen carefully now, and learn how Raven tricks Crow.

Chorus: Winter is coming.
Beware! Beware!
The leaves are falling,
there's a chill in the air.
Winter is coming.
Beware! Beware!
Gather your food,
for no one will share.

Narrator: Long ago, Raven lived up in the mountains by the great river. He was very lazy! In the fall, all the other animals gathered their food for the winter, but Raven played. He laughed at everyone who was working hard.

Crow: Raven, if you don't gather your food now, you will starve this winter. Soon the snow will cover all the food.

Raven: Ha! Ha! Crow, you work too hard! Come fly through the treetops with me. Let's have some fun! I hate to work!

Crow: Do you see how hard Squirrel is working? He is working hard so he will have enough food for the winter.

Raven: I will not starve. I will find food somewhere. I want to fly through the leaves that fall from the trees. You are a fool, Crow! You work too hard!

Chorus: Raven, Raven!
Beware! Beware!
The winds are blowing.
There's a chill in the air!
The rains will come.
The snow will fall.
Very soon, there'll be no food at all!

Narrator: Winter came to the mountains, and Raven was in trouble. He had no food. His stomach was empty and it growled like a bear. He decided to go looking for something to eat.

Raven: Hello, Squirrel! I see you have many pine nuts and seeds. Will you please share them with me?

Squirrel: I worked very hard while you sat and laughed at me. Go find your own food, Raven. I have only enough food for me! Go away!

Narrator: So Raven trudged on through the snow. Next he went to Bear's den.

Raven: Bear! Bear! *(yelling louder)* Bear!! Bear!! Help me! I am starving. Where are you?

Narrator: But Bear was hibernating in his den. He was in a deep, deep sleep. He did not wake up even though Raven yelled his loudest.

Chorus: Foolish Raven!
You laughed, you played.
Your stomach is empty—
what a mistake you made!

Raven: Now who will give me food? Everyone is stingy or sleeping or gone away for the winter. I will starve if I am not clever enough to get some food! But who can I fool? . . . I know! Crow! He is so vain, I know just how to fool him.

Narrator: So Raven went to Crow's house.

Raven: Crow, I hear you are giving a potlatch. Winter has come and it is cold. You are so kind to have such a grand celebration for all the animals. It will be so much fun. Everyone is very excited. They know you will have lots of tasty food.

Crow: I am not planning a potlatch. Who told you I was having a celebration?

Raven: Everyone says you are. Hurry and start fixing the food. Don't forget to practice your songs. We all love your singing! Your songs are the most beautiful in all the forest.

Crow: They want me to sing? No one likes my singing. All the animals say I sound terrible.

Raven: Oh, yes, they do love your singing! Your voice is wonderful. Everyone wants to hear you sing.

Crow: Really? Do you really like my singing?

Raven: Oh, yes, I love to hear your sweet, sweet voice.

Narrator: Now Crow loved to sing, but he did have a terrible voice. No one wanted to hear him sing. But he was foolish and vain, and so he believed Raven.

Crow: They like my singing! I will give a wonderful potlatch with lots of food and I will sing for everyone. I will make them very happy!

Narrator: So Crow worked hard preparing food for his guests. He used all the food he had stored for the winter. Meanwhile, Raven rushed around inviting all the animals. He told them that it was HIS potlatch. Later on, Raven returned to Crow's house. As he drew near, he could hear Crow singing. It sounded terrible!

Raven: Crow, everyone is coming! They are excited to attend your potlatch. Be sure to cook enough food for everyone! They will be very hungry. They are anxious to hear your wonderful songs.

Narrator: When the animals arrived, Raven welcomed them to his potlatch. Crow was busy cooking and singing. He did not hear Raven tell the animals that it was HIS potlatch.

Raven: Welcome to my potlatch, Deer. Come in and enjoy my wonderful food.

Deer: It smells yummy! Thank you for inviting me to your celebration.

Raven: Welcome, Rabbit. Come in and enjoy my potlatch.

Rabbit: This looks like a wonderful party. You have worked so hard, Raven. Look at all the beautiful food you have prepared. Thank you for inviting me.

Narrator: Crow entertained the guests with one song after another. As he came to the end of one song, Raven asked him to sing another. Crow barely got a bite to eat, and soon his voice grew hoarse.

Raven: Crow, your voice has gone hoarse. Please rest while I take care of your guests.

Narrator: And so Raven prepared the leftover food to send home with the guests, according to potlatch tradition. You can imagine who took home more food than anyone else, right? Yes, of course! It was Raven. And so Crow soon found himself alone in his empty home.

Crow: I'm so tired from all that cooking and singing. I barely ate a bite, and not even a morsel of food is left here for me! But I am not worried. I know my friends will soon invite me to a potlatch at their homes since I threw such a wonderful party!

Narrator: But Crow did not get invited to his friends' homes. Do you know why? Of course, because all the animals thought it was Raven who had invited them to the grand potlatch.

Raven: Now I have enough food to keep me full for a while! After that, the other animals will invite me to their homes for dinner. They owe it to me for coming to my grand potlatch.

Narrator: And so while Raven spent the winter enjoying one feast after another, Crow spent it looking for scraps and crying in his hoarse voice. His voice never really did come back. You can still hear him squawking, "Caw! Caw! Caw!" And you can still see him looking for his potlatch leftovers.

Name _____

Plan a Potlatch

A **potlatch** is a grand party given by a person or a family. It can take a year or even longer to plan a potlatch. The host must plan the food, games, dancing, singing, and gifts for the guests.

Imagine you are going to give a potlatch. Use this form to plan your party.

Guests

_____

_____

_____

_____

Food

_____

_____

_____

_____

Activities

_____

_____

_____

_____

Gifts

_____

_____

_____

_____

Name _____

Crow's Potlatch—
An Accordion Book

Students may use the accordion book they create to retell "Crow's Potlatch."

Materials (for each student)

- 6" x 18" (15 x 45.5 cm) white construction paper
- copy of the student directions (bottom portion of page 25)
- crayons or colored pencils, scissors, glue

Teacher Directions

Guide students in following these directions:

1. Fold the white construction paper in half two times.
2. Fold each short edge back to the first fold.
3. Write the title "Crow's Potlatch" on the front page.
4. Cut out and order the four sections of text.
5. Glue the text along the bottom of the four book pages.
6. Color a picture on each page to illustrate the words.

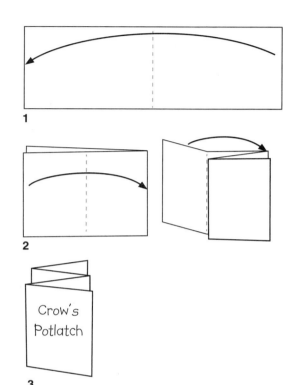

1

2

Crow's
Potlatch

3

1. Cut apart   2. Paste in order   3. Color a picture

The animals had a good time at the potlatch. They took all of the extra food home with them.	**Crow had no food and no voice. All he could say was, "Caw! Caw! Caw!"**
Raven tricked Crow into having a potlatch. All the animals came. Raven told them it was HIS party.	**Raven played while Crow and all the other animals gathered food for the winter.**

Now Presenting...

Earth's Seven Continents

Each of the seven continents on Earth is unique. Each has its own habitats, creatures, and cultures. This rhyming script introduces some of these features.

Setting the Stage

Background

Use a map to point out and introduce each continent, as well as the other sites mentioned in the script. You may need to give additional information about landmarks that are unfamiliar to your students, such as the Great Wall of China (the only human-made object on Earth visible from space), the Alps (a mountain range that crosses Europe), Big Ben (a famous clock tower in London, England), the Danube (a river that runs through Germany, Austria, Slovakia, Hungary, Yugoslavia, Bulgaria, Romania, and Russia), etc.

Staging

Consider holding up maps or large cutouts of each continent as its description is read. You might assign students to create and present sound effects for the animals that are mentioned.

Vocabulary

Introduce and discuss the following words before reading the script:

absurd: not true; ridiculous

bold: brave; courageous

canopy: a covering of treetops

culture: the customs, arts, and ways of the people of a particular time and place

glacier: a large mass of ice that moves slowly down a mountain or valley

grand: large and very special in appearance

terrain: ground; land

varied: different; changing; not all the same

vast: immense; very large

wander: to move here and there

wonder: something remarkable

Now Presenting...

Earth's Seven Continents

Meet Earth's seven continents as each one tells you about some of the special features that make it unique.

Characters

Narrator .... _____

_____

Asia .... _____

_____

Africa .... _____

_____

North America .... _____

_____

South America .... _____

_____

Antarctica .... _____

_____

Europe .... _____

_____

Australia .... _____

_____

27

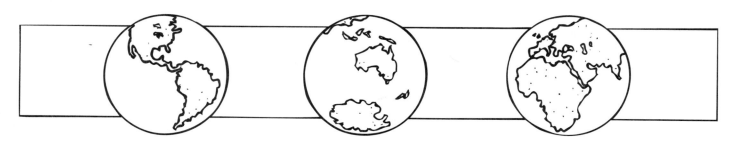

Earth's Seven Continents

Narrator   South America
Asia   Antarctica
Africa   Europe
North America   Australia

Narrator: There are seven continents on Earth,
seven great masses of land.
Some are large and some are small,
but each one has something grand.

Asia is the largest,
and Africa's number two.
North America is third in size,
between two oceans blue.

South America is in fourth place.
Antarctica is number five.
Europe is the second to last,
and Australia is smallest in size.

There are seven continents on Earth,
seven great masses of land.
Some are large and some are small,
but each one has something grand.

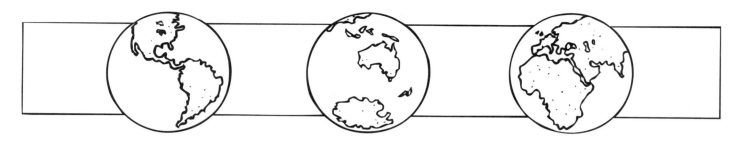

Asia: The continent of Asia
is the largest of them all,
with over fifty countries
and the longest wall.
There's Cambodia and Vietnam,
Japan and India, too.
There's Thailand and Korea,
just to name a few.
More people live in Asia
than in all the other lands.
There's so much there to see and do,
so much that's fine and grand!

Africa: Though Africa is next in size,
some say that it's the best.
Drums and dancers pound a beat
from the East Coast to the West.
You can see the Congo River
and the Serengeti Plain.
Lions, giraffes, and zebras
all wander this terrain.
Earth hides riches deep beneath
this vast and varied land.
Gold and diamonds sparkle bright,
as does Sahara sand.

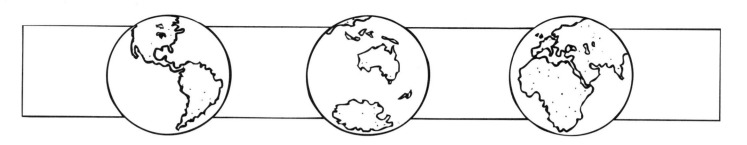

North America: Our own North America
is the third in size.
Its canyons, plains, and mountains
are all wonders that we prize.
From Panama to Canada,
from Mexico to Maine,
people share and cultures mix—
none are quite the same.
There are grizzly bears and moose,
coyotes, seals, and quail.
And along those long, long coastlines
you might even see a whale!

South America: South America is fourth in size,
with emerald jungles and bright blue skies.
The Amazon River flows far and long,
where birds and beasts all sing their song.
A sloth climbs slowly through a tree,
monkeys swing in the canopy.
Up in the Andes Mountains high,
the Incas lived in days gone by.
Coffee and chocolate, potatoes and gum,
are foods that from South America come.

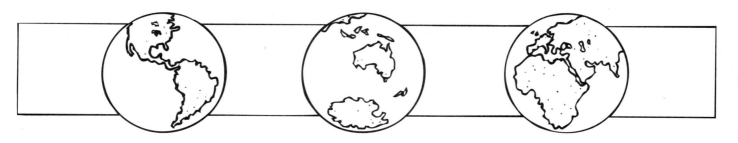

Antarctica: Antarctica is fifth in size.
It's a desert of ice where glaciers rise.
You'll find penguins and seals, whales and birds,
but a polar bear would be absurd!
Explorers and scientists must be bold
to visit that sub-zero cold.
No countries or cities or towns are here,
no roads, no cars, no TVs near.
It's a land that is covered with ice and snow,
a land where few would choose to go.

Europe: The sixth is Europe; it's second to last.
Here you'll find castles and tales from the past.
You can pick tulips in Holland and olives in Spain.
You can skate on the Danube, or ride on a train.
There are wolves in the forest, hedgehogs in the row.
There are sights and sounds that travelers love so.
You can see the Eiffel Tower or listen to Big Ben,
eat some tasty pasta or have teatime with a friend.

Australia: Australia's way down under,
the smallest of the seven.
The outback wilds are home to
the oddest creatures under heaven!
There's the platypus with beak and fur,
the hopping kangaroo,
the cuddly, cute koala bear,
just to name a few.
There are big waves for the surfers
and big reefs for the fish.
If you catch yourself a crocodile,
you can try a tasty dish!

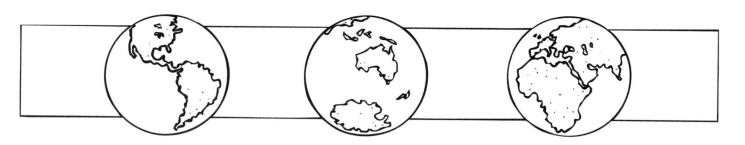

Narrator: There are seven continents on Earth,
seven great masses of land.
Some are large and some are small,
but each one has something grand.

Asia is the largest,
and Africa's number two.
North America is third in size,
between two oceans blue.

South America is in fourth place.
Antarctica is number five.
Europe is the second to last,
and Australia is smallest in size.

Name _____

The Seven Continents

Write the names of the continents and oceans on the map.
Color each continent a different color.

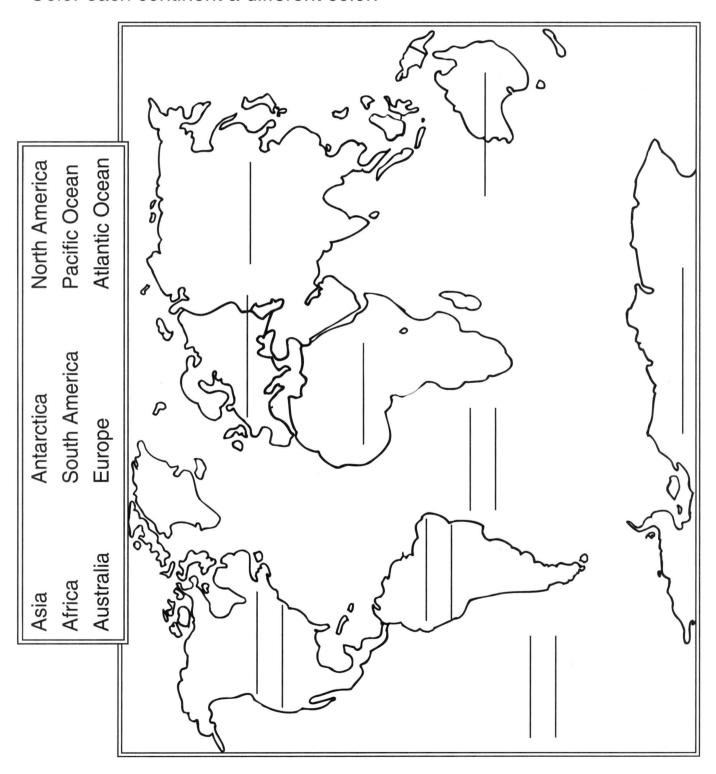

North America
Pacific Ocean
Atlantic Ocean

Antarctica
South America
Europe

Asia
Africa
Australia

Readers' Theater, Grade 2 • EMC 3307

Name _____

Seven Continents Word Search

Find two words from each continent.

Africa	**Antarctica**	**South America**	**Asia**
diamond	ice	monkey	Japan
zebra	penguin	Amazon	wall
Australia	**Europe**	**North America**	
crocodile	Holland	coyote	
kangaroo	wolves	whale	

```
w  o  l  v  e  s  m  a  r  z  i  q  u  o  t
u  k  a  o  s  t  o  x  e  c  o  y  o  t  e
z  a  f  j  w  r  n  d  i  a  m  o  n  d  s
e  n  e  a  h  z  k  r  a  t  o  b  l  u  h
i  g  r  p  a  e  e  p  e  n  g  u  i  n  y
h  a  x  a  l  b  y  w  o  l  q  i  x  e  o
g  r  o  n  e  r  s  m  h  o  l  l  a  n  d
t  o  n  s  u  a  w  i  y  x  w  a  l  l  r
y  o  k  a  m  a  z  o  n  i  t  y  o  r  u
i  c  e  q  u  b  c  r  o  c  o  d  i  l  e
```

Now Presenting...

Febold Feboldson Saves Nebraska from Drought

Febold Feboldson, a mighty unusual man, settled in Nebraska when all the other folks were heading West. He saved Nebraska from grasshoppers, cyclones, and in this tale, even from drought!

Setting the Stage

Background

A Nebraska lumberman named Wayne Carroll created the tall tale character Febold Feboldson. His stories were published in newspapers in Gothenburg, Nebraska, between 1923 and 1933. Febold used clever thinking to tackle the seemingly insurmountable problems posed by the harsh conditions on the plains in the hope of encouraging people traveling West to stay and settle in Nebraska.

You may wish to point out to students that the humorous exaggerations in the Febold Feboldson stories are characteristic of the tall tale genre. Use "The Water Cycle" activity on page 41 to review the cycle with students before reading the script.

Encore

Share other fantastic tales of Febold Feboldson with students in books such as *Febold Feboldson* by Ariane Dewey and *American Tall Tales* by Mary Pope Osborne.

Vocabulary

Introduce and discuss the following words before reading the script:

barren: not able to produce very much; not fertile

bold: without fear; showing courage

bonfire: a fire built outdoors

clover: a small green plant with three leaves

evaporate: to turn from water into vapor

introduce: to bring into practice or use

Nebraska: one of the midwestern states in the United States

settle: to be among the first to begin to live in a new place

Now Presenting...

Febold Feboldson Saves Nebraska from Drought

Times are bad in Nebraska! The skies are clear, the days are hot, and the rain is nowhere to be seen. Who will save the land from drought?

Characters

Storyteller .... _____

Febold .... _____

Pioneer Father .... _____

Pioneer Mother .... _____

Pioneer Boy .... _____

Pioneer Girl .... _____

Pioneers .... _____

_____

_____

Febold Feboldson
Saves Nebraska from Drought

······················ **Characters** ······················

Storyteller
Febold
Pioneer Father
Pioneer Mother

Pioneer Boy
Pioneer Girl
Pioneers

Storyteller: Howdy, folks! I want to introduce you to a man who lived in Nebraska in the days of long ago. We called him Febold Feboldson. He was smart! He was clever! He was bold! That sure looks like him riding up on his horse now. Yep, here he comes!

Febold: Oh boy! I think I see some folks comin' over that hill yonder. They're probably on their way to California. I sure wish they would stay here. I'm as lonely as a Christmas tree in the middle of the desert.

Father: Hello there, fella!

Febold: Are you folks looking for a place to settle down and start a farm?

Mother: We're goin' West with the wagon train. We're going to start a farm where the grass is as green as clover and the water is as plentiful as ants.

Febold: Why don't you folks settle here? When it rains, this land is as pretty as a picture. I sure would like some neighbors to keep me company.

Mother: This land looks pretty barren to me. There seems to be more dirt in the air than on the ground. This land is as dry as a bone! It sure looks like a drought to me.

Boy: Mama, I'm thirsty! May I have a drink?

Mother: We are pretty short on water. That river over there looks as dirty as your shirts after a day on the trail. It looks like it hasn't rained here in a month of Sundays.

Febold: Well ma'am, I think I might be able to do something about that. If I make it rain, will you folks stay here and be my neighbors?

Father: There sure is a lot of land around here. If there were water, we just might stay.

Febold: I'm going to think a bit about this problem. I'll see what I can come up with.

Storyteller: Febold sat down. He put his big chin in his big hand and thought big thoughts. Febold never gave up on things. He thought and thought. And then he thought some more.

Febold: *(jumping up)* By golly, I've got it! We're going to need lots and lots of wood! I mean LOTS and LOTS!

Girl: *(excited)* Everyone, help us! We've got to find wood! *(pause)* Why do we need wood?

Febold: You'll soon see! Before you know it, it will be raining as hard as if you were standing under a powerful waterfall.

Storyteller: Now, all those folks in the wagon train went out lookin' for wood. They had to look hard and long to find it.

Children: We found some wood,
we knew that we could!
We looked here and there.
We looked darn near everywhere!

The land is so dry,
we thought we might fry.
Make the rain come right away.
Turn the sky from blue to gray!

Father: That pile of wood we made is as big as a mountain.

Febold: Now I'm going to take that wood and build bonfires all along this miserable river.

Girl: Why are you going to do that?

Febold: I'm going to light these bonfires up and down this river. The fires are going to be as hot as lava from a volcano. What do you think will happen to the water in that river when those bonfires are blazing?

Boy: I don't know . . . It sure will get hot!

Febold: Watch what happens when this water gets hot! I'm going to make it rain!

Storyteller: Next, Febold lit all the bonfires. They sure got hot! The water in that miserable old river got so hot that it evaporated away into mist. Big clouds started to form in the sky. Those clouds were getting so big and full, it looked like they were balloons that were going to burst any minute.

Mother: Look, look at the sky! It's filling up with clouds. They look like giant gray cream puffs floating around up there.

Boy: Those clouds are getting mighty big. They're bumping into each other.

Girl: I hear thunder! I see lightning! It's going to rain!

Children: Febold did it!
He made it rain.
The fires he built
made clouds again.

It sure did rain,
and it sure did pour.
The folks on the plain
were wishing for more!

Febold: Is that enough rain for you? Will you stay? There will be grass as green as clover. Flowers as blue as the summer sky will grow here. Stay, please stay. Be my neighbors. I sure do get lonely out here.

Pioneers: We'll stay! We'll stay! The river is getting full. Now there is water for our horses and crops. Thanks, Febold! You're a mighty fine fellow and a good thinker. You'll make a good neighbor.

Storyteller: So the folks stayed—for a while, anyway. Things were going pretty well. Then those millions of grasshoppers came. But Febold Feboldson, that big thinker who never gave up, well, he took care of them, too! But then, that's another story!

Name _____

The Water Cycle

- Look at the pictures of the water cycle.
- Find the words below that tell about each picture.
- Cut out the words and glue them below the correct picture.

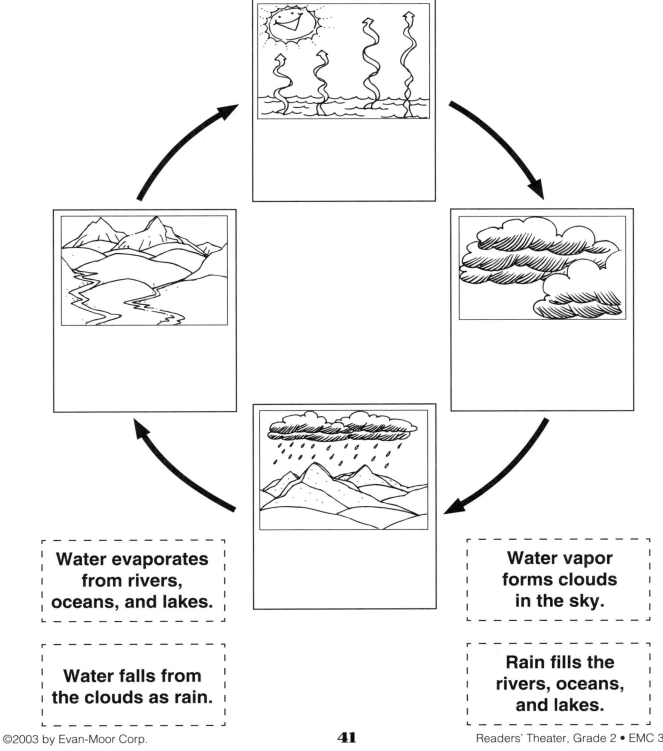

Water evaporates from rivers, oceans, and lakes.

Water vapor forms clouds in the sky.

Water falls from the clouds as rain.

Rain fills the rivers, oceans, and lakes.

Name _____

Truth or Tall Tale?

Some of the events in a tall tale could really be true. Others could only be make-believe.

- Read each sentence.
- If it tells something that could be true, write a **T** next to it.
- If it tells something that could only be make-believe, write an **M**.

_____ 1. Febold Feboldson wanted people to stay in Nebraska.

_____ 2. The plains have more dirt in the air than on the ground.

_____ 3. Febold put his big chin in his big hand and thought.

_____ 4. The pioneers made a pile of wood as high as a mountain.

_____ 5. A fire can make water hot.

_____ 6. Rain clouds are really great big cream puffs.

_____ 7. Sometimes there is lightning with a rainstorm.

_____ 8. We hear thunder when clouds crash into each other.

_____ 9. You can use river water for growing crops.

_____ 10. Life is not so lonely when you have nice neighbors.

Colorful Descriptions

This tall tale about Febold Feboldson uses lots of colorful descriptions. Find each of the phrases below in the script, and then complete them using the words you found.

1. Flowers were as blue as _____.

2. The water was as plentiful as _____.

3. The grass was as green as _____.

Choose the best word to complete each description.

feather
ice
thunder
night
pancake
honey
bee

4. As dark as _____.

5. As sweet as _____.

6. As busy as a _____.

7. As flat as a _____.

8. As cold as _____.

9. As light as a _____.

10. As loud as _____.

Now write two sentences of your own. Use some of the colorful descriptions on this page.

11. _____

_____

12. _____

_____

Now Presenting...

The Statue of Liberty

The Statue of Liberty is finally in place, and the unveiling is about to begin. A newscaster interviews important figures of the day as we learn more about this impressive monument.

Setting the Stage

Background

Before you read the script, share information about the history of the Statue of Liberty with your students. Tell them that in the 1860s, a French lawyer named Edouard de Laboulaye wanted to give the people of the United States a gift from the people of France. He wanted to give them something to honor the freedom and liberty that was so important to both countries. He asked the French sculptor Frederic Auguste-Bartholdi to help him with his idea. Bartholdi visited New York and saw Bedloe's Island. He thought it would be the perfect place for a statue. The people of France raised the money to build the statue. The people of the United States raised the money to build its base. Bartholdi's Statue of Liberty was finally presented to the people of the United States on October 28, 1886.

Staging

Set up one area of the stage for the dialog that takes place in the family's home. Another area may represent the harbor area, and a third area may represent Bedloe's Island, where the interviews take place.

Encore

For more information on the making of the Statue of Liberty, read *The Story of the Statue of Liberty* by Betsy and Giulio Maestro and *Liberty* by Lynn Curlee.

Vocabulary

Introduce and discuss the following words before reading the script:

accomplish: to carry out

base: the part on which something else rests; the bottom

copper: a reddish metal that is easy to work with

crate: a large box made for shipping something

design: a drawing or plan used as a pattern for creating something

donate: to give

liberty: freedom

magnificent: grand; splendid

newscaster: a radio announcer who presents news programs

pedestal: the base that a statue stands on

statue: the image of someone or something carved in stone or wood, or cast in bronze

unveil: to uncover, often in a special ceremony

Now Presenting...

The Statue of Liberty

The Statue of Liberty has finally been erected on Bedloe's Island. Join the celebration for its dedication!

Characters

Narrator.................................... _____

Jack (an American child).......... _____

Mr. Simpson (Jack's father) ...... _____

Sally (Jack's older sister) .... _____

Newscaster .... _____

Frederic-Auguste Bartholdi .... _____
(French sculptor)

Captain of the ship *Isere* .... _____

President Grover Cleveland...... _____

Speaker 1.................................. _____

Speaker 2.................................. _____

Speaker 3.................................. _____

Speaker 4.................................. _____

The Statue of Liberty

························· **Characters** ·························

Narrator
Jack
Mr. Simpson
Sally
Newscaster
Frederic-Auguste Bartholdi

Captain of the ship *Isere*
President Grover Cleveland
Speaker 1
Speaker 2
Speaker 3
Speaker 4

Narrator: This story takes place in New York City on October 28, 1886. The city is celebrating the unveiling of the Statue of Liberty.

Jack: Dad, Dad! This is a great parade! Look at all that paper flying out of the windows. It looks like white ribbons. I'm glad there is no school today! This is the most exciting day of my life!

Mr. Simpson: This is a special day! The Statue of Liberty is finally finished. Today we will be able to see what it looks like.

Sally: And we helped! I gave 10¢ to help pay for the base that was built for the statue. Jack gave 10¢, too. It was fun to see my name in Mr. Pulitzer's newspaper. There must have been a thousand names!

Mr. Simpson: Mr. Pulitzer also helped a lot. He gave $1,000 for the base of the statue. It cost $100,000 to build.

Sally: Jeepers! That's a lot of money!

Jack: Come on, Sally! Dad said we can go down to the harbor!

Narrator: Sally, Jack, and Mr. Simpson rush off to the harbor.

(at the harbor)

Jack: Look at all the people! Look at all the boats!

Sally: Dad, I can see the statue out there on Bedloe's Island! It's still covered up. Wow, is it ever big! I'm so glad people gave enough money to finish the base.

Mr. Simpson: Yes, some people thought the statue would never be put up because they ran out of money. We are lucky that so many people donated money, just like you did.

Narrator: Sally, Jack, and their father watch the celebration from the harbor. Hundreds more fill the island.

(The action shifts to Bedloe's Island.)

Newscaster: This is the big day! We are on Bedloe's Island in New York City Harbor. It is October 28, 1886. President Grover Cleveland is here. Most of the people in New York City are here! And here comes Mr. Bartholdi, the man who designed this grand statue . . . Mr. Bartholdi, will you tell us about this magnificent statue?

Mr. Bartholdi: The dream of my life is accomplished! The statue is finally finished. The people of France are so happy. They have finally given their present to the people of the United States. It has taken lots of hard work and it cost a great deal of money to build.

Newscaster: Did you design the statue by yourself?

Bartholdi: No, no! Many people helped me. Mr. Eiffel designed the inside of the statue so it would be strong. It has a skeleton of steel inside. It is made of copper on the outside.

Newscaster: How long did it take to build?

Bartholdi: I started designing the statue in 1871. It was not finished until 1884.

Newscaster: That was 13 years! That is a long time.

Bartholdi: Yes, it took 13 years and many people to build this beautiful statue. We built it in Paris so everyone could see it. Then we took it apart so we could send it here.

Newscaster: Thank you, Mr. Bartholdi. We hope you have a safe journey back to France . . . And here is the Captain of the *Isere,* the ship that brought the statue. Captain, how did you get the statue here from France?

Captain: It was taken apart and then packed into 214 crates. Each piece was numbered so it could be put back together, just like a puzzle. We had to load all the crates onto our ship. When we got to New York, 214 crates had to be unloaded. It was a lot of work!

Newscaster: Thank you, Captain. I see President Grover Cleveland is ready to give his speech now. Let's listen to what he says.

President Grover Cleveland: This is a very special day. We thank all the American people who gave money for the building of the pedestal. We thank all the people of France for giving us this beautiful statue. Lady Liberty is a symbol of freedom. She will welcome all the immigrants who come to this country looking for liberty.

Narrator: Here are some facts about the Statue of Liberty:

Speaker 1: The Statue of Liberty is 305 feet tall.

Speaker 2: Lady Liberty's mouth is 3 feet wide.

Speaker 3: Each eye is $2\frac{1}{2}$ feet across.

Speaker 4: Her index finger is 8 feet long.

Speaker 1: The entire statue weighs 450,000 pounds.

Speaker 2: The tablet she is holding has the date July 4, 1776 written on it.

Speaker 3: Lady Liberty's crown has seven spikes, one for each of the seven continents.

Speaker 4: In her right hand, she holds a flaming torch to welcome all newcomers to the United States.

Speaker 1: There are 354 steps up to her crown. That's about the same as 22 stories!

Newscaster: Now it's time for the unveiling. It looks like Mr. Bartholdi will be pulling the cord. Here it goes!

Sally: Goodness gracious! Her face is so beautiful!

Newscaster: Well, folks, the lady has been unveiled! She stands in our harbor to welcome all. This has been a day we'll never forget!

The Statue of Liberty

The Statue of Liberty was taken apart for the trip from France to the United States. All the pieces were numbered. The numbers helped workers put the statue back together.

- Cut apart the pieces of the statue.

- Use the numbers to help you put the pieces together correctly.

- Glue the pieces on a 6" x 18" (15 x 45.5 cm) sheet of paper.

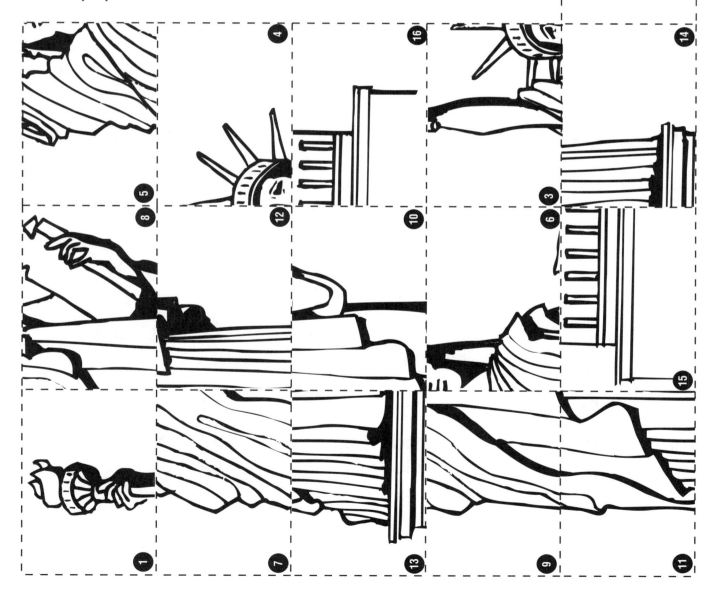

Name _____

Remembering Lady Liberty

See what you can remember about the play. Circle the correct answers.

1. Which country gave the Statue of Liberty to the United States?

   England   France   Spain

2. Who designed the Statue of Liberty?

   Mr. Bartholdi   Mr. Eiffel   Mr. Pulitzer

3. In what year was the statue unveiled?

   1990   1389   1886

4. How many spikes are on Lady Liberty's crown?

   four   ten   seven

5. What date is written on the tablet that Lady Liberty holds?

   January 1, 2003   July 4, 1776   October 28, 1886

Name _____

Statue Math

Read each problem. Circle the correct answer or write it below.

1. If you can climb 100 steps in 5 minutes, about how long do you think it would take to climb the 354 steps in the Statue of Liberty?

   18 minutes   1 hour   3 hours   45 minutes

2. It costs $7.00 for adults and $3.00 for children to ride the ferry to the Statue of Liberty. How much would it cost for Sally, Jack, and their father to ride the ferry?

   $30.00 $10.00 $13.00 $7.00

3. Lady Liberty's finger is 8 feet long. Find something that is about 8 feet long. Use your ruler or a yardstick to help you measure. What did you find?

   _____

4. Mr. Bartholdi was born in 1834. He started planning the Statue of Liberty in 1876. How old was Mr. Bartholdi when he started working on the statue?

   34 years old   21 years old   42 years old   52 years old

5. The amount of copper used in the statue was 179,200 pounds. The amount of steel used in the statue was 250,000 pounds. How much did the copper and steel weigh in all?

   429,200 pounds   294,200 pounds   329,200 pounds

Now Presenting...

The Foolish Little Hare: A Fable

"The Foolish Little Hare" is an Indian variation of the European "Chicken Little" story. In the Indian fable, a little hare fears that the earth will crack and swallow him up. When a loud cracking sound awakens the hare from a dream, he alarms other animals in the jungle.

Setting the Stage

Background

Remind students that fables are stories that teach lessons. Often the characters in fables are animals. Tell students that this fable is from India.

Staging

Students may create simple headbands with the ears of their character on them. You may wish to have them write the name of their animal character across the front of the headband.

Encore

To read another version of this fable with children, try Rafe Martin's "Foolish Rabbit's Big Mistake," featuring beautiful art by Ed Young. You may also enjoy comparing the story to any version of the "Chicken Little" story. Compare the two tales using a Venn diagram.

Vocabulary

Introduce and discuss the following words before reading the script:

foolish: unwise; not having good sense

hare: an animal similar to a rabbit

lumber: to walk very heavily

The Foolish Little Hare: A Fable

A foolish little hare is always fearful. He fears the earth will crack open and swallow him up. When he hears a cracking sound, he rushes to warn the other animals that the earth will soon swallow them up.

Characters

Narrator.. _____

Foolish Little Hare .... _____

Hare 1 .... _____

Hare 2 .... _____

Hare 3 .... _____

Deer .... _____

Tiger... _____

Elephant...................................... _____

Lion King .... _____

Monkey 1 .... _____

Monkey 2 .... _____

The Foolish Little Hare: A Fable

···················· **Characters** ····················

Narrator	Monkey 2
Foolish Little Hare	Deer
Hare 1	Tiger
Hare 2	Elephant
Hare 3	King Lion
Monkey 1	

Narrator: Once, far away and long ago in the country of India, there lived a very foolish little hare. He always expected terrible things to happen.

Foolish Little Hare: What will I do? What will I do? What if the clouds fall and crush me? What if the earth cracks open and swallows me up? What will I do? What will I do?

Hare 1: Why do you worry so much little hare? The clouds are not going to fall on you and crush you. The earth is not going to crack open and swallow you! You are a silly hare.

Hare 2: I think you should rest. Take a nap and stop thinking about these terrible things.

Narrator: And so the little hare lay down under the coconut trees and took a nap. He slept deeply while the monkeys played in the trees above him. They loved to play catch with the coconuts.

Monkey 1: I love this coconut tree. It always has so many coconuts. Catch!

Monkey 2: Oops! I missed that one. You threw it too fast!

Narrator: The coconut crashed to the ground and broke open near the foolish little hare.

Foolish Little Hare: What was that? What was that? Oh no! I heard a crack! The earth is cracking open and I will be swallowed up. I must run as fast as I can.

Hare 1: Why are you running so fast, Foolish Little Hare?

Foolish Little Hare: The earth is cracking open. I will be swallowed up if I don't run away.

Hare 2: What? The earth is cracking? We must run, too. We cannot let the earth swallow us. Run! Run! Run!

Narrator: The hares ran as fast as they could. Soon they passed another hare.

Hare 3: Where are you going so fast? Why are you running?

Foolish Little Hare: We are running because the earth is cracking open. It is going to swallow us up!

Hare 3: The earth is cracking! Oh no! I must run or I will fall into the crack and be swallowed by the earth.

Narrator: The hares ran as fast as they could. Soon they came to where Deer was grazing on the soft, cool grass.

Deer: Hares! Hares! Why are you running so fast? Is the panther after you?

All Hares: No, it is not the panther! The earth is cracking! We are running fast so we will not be swallowed up.

Deer: Then I must run, too. I do not want the earth to swallow me up!

Narrator: Soon the hares and the deer came to a very large tiger who was resting near a tree.

Tiger: Why are you all running so fast?

Deer: We are running because the earth is cracking open and it is going to swallow us up! Hurry or it will swallow you!

Tiger: Oh, dear me! I do not want to be swallowed up by the earth! I shall have to run fast.

Narrator: And so the hares, the deer, and the tiger ran as fast as they could. In a little while they came upon Elephant.

Elephant: STOP! STOP! Tell me why you are all running so fast!

Tiger: We are running so the earth will not swallow us up. The earth is cracking open!

Elephant: The earth is cracking? I do not want to be swallowed up! I will run with you! Wait for me.

Narrator: Soon all the animals were thundering through the jungle. The elephant came lumbering behind. The wise Lion King was resting on a clump of grass, looking out over his lands when he saw all the animals running like the wind. He raced ahead of them and roared.

Lion King: STOP! What are you doing? Why are you running like the wind?

All animals: The earth is cracking open! The earth will swallow us all if we do not run away.

Lion King: Phooey! Who told you the earth is cracking? We must take time to find out if such a thing is true. Who is it that saw the earth cracking? Elephant?

Elephant: Not I! Ask Tiger! He told me!

Tiger: Not I! Ask Deer! She told me!

Deer: Not I! Ask the hares! They told me!

All Hares: Not us! We did not see the earth cracking! It was Foolish Little Hare who told us.

Lion King: Foolish Little Hare, what made you think the earth was cracking?

Foolish Little Hare: I heard it crack!

Lion King: Where did you hear it crack?

Foolish Little Hare: I was fast asleep by the big coconut tree when a loud cracking sound woke me up. It was as loud as thunder. "The earth is cracking open," I thought, so I ran away as fast as I could. I do not want the earth to swallow me up.

Lion King: We must go back and see where the earth is cracking.

Foolish Little Hare: I am not going back there! Nothing can make me go back there!

Lion King: I will take you on my back. I will keep you safe.

Narrator: The foolish little hare crawled slowly onto the lion's back. He did not really want to go back to the coconut tree. All the animals followed Lion King and Foolish Little Hare back to the coconut tree. When they got there, the monkeys were still busy tossing coconuts to each other in the treetops. Just then, a coconut fell and hit the earth with a loud CRACK.

Lion King: You see, Foolish Little Hare? That sound was not the earth cracking open. It was a coconut splitting apart on the ground.

Foolish Little Hare: The earth is not cracking? It was only a coconut? Then I suppose I can go back and finish my nap now.

Deer: You foolish little hare!

Lion King: All you other animals are foolish, too. You must not believe everything you are told. You must find out for yourselves what is true and what is not.

Narrator: And so Foolish Little Hare went back to the coconut tree to rest. All the other animals went back to munching and chewing, taking long naps, and playing with their friends. And they never forgot that you cannot always believe what you hear. You must find out for yourself what is true.

Jungle Crossword Puzzle

Read the clues and then choose the best word to complete each sentence. Write your answer on the puzzle.

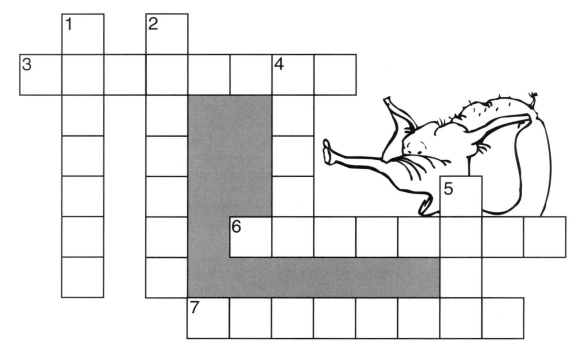

Across

3. The monkeys dropped _____ to the ground.
6. Foolish Little Hare thought the earth was _____.
7. The _____ lumbered along after all the other animals.

Down

1. The _____ were playing in the tree.
2. Foolish Little Hare was _____.
4. The _____ told the elephant that the earth was cracking open.
5. The _____ showed the animals that the earth was not cracking open.

Word Box

cracking

monkeys

foolish

lion

tiger

elephant

coconuts

Name _____

Some Friendly Advice

Use this page to write a letter to Foolish Little Hare. Give him some helpful advice about learning the truth.

_____
Date

_____,

_____

_____

_____

_____

_____

_____

_____

_____

_____

_____

Sincerely,

_____

Now Presenting...

Don't Forget Zero

Zero is a very important placeholder in our number system. As students combine digits to create numbers, they realize that zero is a must!

Setting the Stage

Background

Understanding place value and the use of zero is a challenge for young children. This script gives helpful examples to support children in understanding the importance of zero in making numbers.

Staging

Line up 10 chairs at the front of the class for students representing the numerals. Attach each numeral's script to a piece of construction paper with the corresponding numeral printed boldly on it for the audience to see. Be sure students show their numerals as indicated in the script whenever their numeral is featured.

Encore

This would be an ideal time to introduce two books by Betsy Franco: *What's Zero?* and *Counting Caterpillars and Other Math Poems.*

Vocabulary

Introduce and discuss the following words before reading the script:

digit: any of the figures 0, 1, 2, 3, 4, 5, 6, 7, 8, 9

numeral: a figure or group of figures that stand for a number

placeholder: something that keeps a space available

zero: the symbol or numeral 0, which represents the complete absence of any quantity

Now Presenting...

Don't Forget Zero

Zero is a very important placeholder in our number system. As you combine digits to create numerals, you will see that zero is a must!

Characters

One .... _____

Two .... _____

Three .... _____

Four .... _____

Five .... _____

Six .... _____

Seven .... _____

Eight .... _____

Nine .... _____

Zero .... _____

Teacher .... _____

Child 1 .... _____

Child 2 .... _____

Child 3 .... _____

Don't Forget Zero

········· **Characters** ·········

One	Eight
Two	Nine
Three	Zero
Four	Teacher
Five	Child 1
Six	Child 2
Seven	Child 3

One: Is everybody ready? We have to hurry over to that school today and answer the children's questions. Are you ready, Two?

Two: *(holding up number card)* Two's ready!

Three: *(holding up number card)* Three's ready!

Four: *(holding up number card)* Four's here!

Five: *(holding up number card)* Five's ready.

Six: *(holding up number card)* Six is ready, and here come Seven and Eight.

Nine: And I'm Number Nine. Well, I guess we're all here! Let's get moving. We have work to do.

One: Wait, wait! Where is Zero?

Eight: Oh, we don't need him! He isn't worth anything anyway.

One: Are you sure?

Five: I'm sure. Zero is nothing, and who needs nothing? Come on, let's go.

(All the numbers walk around in a circle and stop. They stand in a line from one to nine.)

Numbers One through Nine: Here we are! Is this the right room?

Teacher: Yes, you've found the right place. Thank you for coming today. Come in and sit down.

Three: What questions do you children have for us today?

Child 1: I'd like to know how many eggs there are in a dozen.

One: Oh boy! I get to go first. *(One moves in front of the other numbers.)*

Two: And I'm right here with you. *(Two stands to the left of One.)*

Teacher: That looks like 12 to me. Is that correct? Are there 12 eggs in a dozen? *(Let audience answer.)*

Teacher: Good job! Who has the next question?

Child 2: I'd like to know how many hours there are in a day.

Four: Oh boy! I get to be in this one! *(moves forward)*

Two: But I have to go first. Move over, Four!

Teacher: That looks like 24. Children, is that how many hours there are in a day? *(Let audience answer.)* Good for you, Two and Four!

Five: I want a turn!

Child 3: Then maybe you can tell me what 10 plus 50 is.

Six: Finally! It's my turn! Let me up here!

Teacher: Are you all alone? I just see a six. But 10 plus 50 can't possibly equal six, can it? *(Let audience answer.)*

Six: Well, I can't do this all by myself. Who is going to help me?

Five and One: Can we help you? Here, let us stand with you. *(Five and One stand side by side.)*

Teacher: Nice effort, but one plus five is not the same as 10 plus 50, is it? *(Let audience answer.)*

One: See? I knew it! We really did need Zero. Zero might be a big nothing, but he sure is important!

Six: Yeah. I need him to stand in the ones place so I can be in the tens place. Then we'll have the right answer.

Seven: I'll go find Zero. We'll be right back.

Eight: Look, here they come! Here is Zero. *(Zero joins the group of numbers.)*

Zero: Why didn't you wait for me?

One: They thought we didn't need you.

Zero: Well, I may be worth nothing, but I'm very important! I can hold a place. I can make all you other numbers worth more!

Teacher: I'm glad you're here, Zero. Now we can answer the question! What is 10 plus 50?

Six: Here we go again! You need me for this answer.

Zero: AND you need me for this answer! *(Zero stands to the left of Six, creating the numeral 60.)*

Teacher: Yes! The answer is 60. Now you've got it. Well, we have time for just one last question. Are you ready?

All Numbers: Yes, we're ready!

Child 4: I'd like to know what two quarters are worth.

Five: *(stepping forward)* My turn! My turn! My turn!

Teacher: Are two quarters worth five? *(Let audience answer.)*

Five: Wake up, Zero! Where are you when I need you?

Zero: *(jumping forward)* Sorry! I was just thinking about . . . nothing. *(Zero stands to Five's left to make the numeral 50.)*

Teacher: That's right! Two quarters are worth 50 cents. You numbers are amazing.

Nine: Yes, we all work together to answer questions and help people figure things out.

Zero: And without me, things just wouldn't add up!

Numbers Everywhere!

See if you can answer the following questions. If you don't know the answer, ask one of your classmates. If there is a zero in the answer, trace the zero with a red crayon. Trace all the other numbers in blue.

1. How many days are there in a week? _____

2. How many months are there in a year? _____

3. How many days are there in a year? _____

4. How many hours are there in a day? _____

5. How many fingers and toes do you have? _____

6. How many pennies are there in a dollar? _____

7. How many sides are there on a triangle? _____

8. How many legs are there on 10 spiders? _____

9. How many nickels are there in a dollar? _____

10. How many numbers are there on a clock? _____

11. How many quarters are there in five dollars? _____

Name _____

Numbers, Numbers, Numbers

Write these numerals.

1. one hundred   _____

2. sixty   _____

3. seventy-five   _____

4. eight hundred   _____

5. forty-seven   _____

6. one hundred forty-seven   _____

7. three hundred five   _____

8. seventy-nine   _____

9. seven hundred sixty   _____

10. ninety   _____

11. four hundred ninety   _____

12. one thousand   _____

13. nine hundred sixty-eight   _____

14. sixty-eight   _____

Name _____

What's Your Number?

Color all the numbers with **0** in the **ones** place red.

Color all the numbers with **0** in the **tens** place yellow.

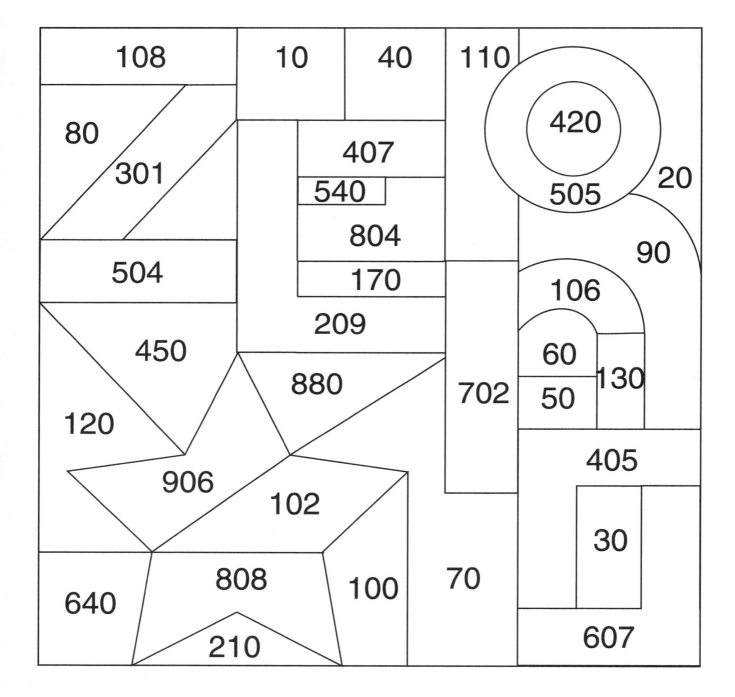

108   10   40   110

80

301

407

540

804

170

420

505

20

90

504

209

106

450

880

60

130

120

702

50

906

405

102

30

640   808   100   70

210   607

What number word do you see? _____

Now Presenting...

How Anansi Brought Stories to Earth

Anansi the spider is a classic trickster character in traditional stories from West Africa. In this tale, Anansi uses his wits once again, this time to obtain the wonderful stories jealously guarded by the sky god.

Setting the Stage

Background

Tell students that stories about Anansi were first told long ago in the West African country now called Ghana. Point out Ghana for them on a map of Africa. Tell students that Anansi is a trickster, and encourage students to mention other familiar tricksters they have read about or heard of (such as Native American characters Raven or Coyote). Explain that Anansi is lazy yet clever, and although he gets into mischief, he always seems to find his way out of it.

Staging

Divide the stage into three areas: one to represent Anansi's home, another to represent the sky god's home, and the third to represent the area where Anansi finds the animals. Provide a long stick (or even a yardstick) for Anansi to hold during his exchange with the python.

Encore

Encourage students to check out other Anansi adventures. Author Eric Kimmel has written several, including *Anansi and the Talking Melon, Anansi Goes Fishing,* and *Anansi and the Moss-Covered Rock.*

Vocabulary

Introduce and discuss the following words before reading the script:

pit: a deep hole in the ground

sap: liquid that circulates through a plant or tree

settle: to come to an agreement about who is right

yam: a sweet potato

Be sure students are familiar with these animals:

hornet: an insect that stings, similar to a bee

leopard: a jungle cat

python: a long, powerful snake

Now Presenting...

How Anansi Brought Stories to Earth

Anansi the spider must capture fierce and dangerous creatures in order to buy the sky god's wonderful stories. How can he meet the sky god's demand and bring the stories back to Earth for all to hear?

Characters

Storyteller 1 .... _____

Storyteller 2 .... _____

Storyteller 3 .... _____

Anansi (the spider) .... _____

Aso (Anansi's wife) .... _____

Nyame (the sky god) .... _____

Onini (the python) .... _____

Osebo (the leopard) .... _____

Mmoboro (the hornet) .... _____

Wee One .... _____

Readers' Theater, Grade 2 • EMC 3307

How Anansi Brought Stories to Earth

············· **Characters** ·············

Storyteller 1   Nyame

Storyteller 2   Onini

Storyteller 3   Osebo

Anansi   Mmoboro

Aso   Wee One

Storyteller 1: Many, many years ago there was a very clever spider. His name was Anansi. Anansi lived in West Africa with his wife, Aso. This is the story of how all the spider stories came to the people of Earth.

Anansi: I am very, very tired. I do wish I could hear a story.

Aso: I do, too. But all the stories belong to Nyame, the sky god.

Anansi: I will go see Nyame. I will ask if I can buy the stories. I will bring them back to Earth. Then all the creatures of Earth will have stories to share.

Storyteller 2: So Anansi went to see Nyame. Others had tried to buy the stories before. But no one had been able to bring Nyame all the things he asked for in return for his stories. Do you think Anansi will be able to?

Nyame: Anansi, what are you doing so far away from home?

Anansi: Nyame, I would like to buy your stories. What price do you ask?

Nyame: You are only a spider! You will not be able to bring me what I want.

Anansi: What must I bring you?

Nyame: I want Onini, the python, who swallows creatures whole. I want Osebo, the leopard, whose teeth are as sharp as spears. I want the Wee One, whom no one ever sees. AND I want Mmoboro, the hornet, whose sting hurts like fire. That is the payment I want for my stories.

Storyteller 3: Now, Anansi was only a little spider. How could he capture these fearsome creatures? Anansi let out his thread and dropped back to Earth. He went to his wife. Listen carefully to hear what Anansi did.

Anansi: Nyame says I am to bring him four things. He wants the python who swallows creatures whole. He wants the leopard whose teeth are as sharp as spears. He wants the Wee One whom no one ever sees. And he wants the hornet, whose sting hurts like fire.

Aso: You are most clever! You can trick the python. Take a palm branch to the river. *(She whispers in Anansi's ear.)*

Anansi: *(At the river, Anansi holds a long branch and seems to argue with himself.)* Yes, it's longer than he is! No! It is not longer than he is! Yes, it is! No, it's not! Yes, it is! No, no, no!! I say, yes!

Onini: Anansi, what are you arguing about?

Anansi: My wife says this palm branch is longer than you are. I say it is not. Can you wrap yourself around it so we can settle our argument? We must know who is right.

Onini: Of courssssssssssse I can!

Anansi: Ah, you are about the same size! Now let me see from this side. Hmm, I'd better look from this side now.

Onini: Anansi, what are you doing?

Anansi: Ha! I am wrapping you up with my thread. Now I will take you to Nyame.

Onini: Help! Help! Anansi, you have tricked me! Someone help me!

Storyteller 3: Soon Anansi stood before Nyame.

Nyame: Anansi, I see you have brought me the python who swallows creatures whole. You are most clever. But can you bring me the leopard whose teeth are as sharp as spears?

Anansi: I will try! I do want your stories so badly.

Storyteller 1: Now, Anansi was only a little spider. How could he capture the leopard whose teeth are as sharp as spears? Anansi let out his thread and dropped back to Earth. He went to his wife. Listen carefully to hear what happened.

Anansi: Now I must capture the leopard whose teeth are as sharp as spears. How shall I do that?

Aso: You can catch the leopard by digging a big pit. *(She whispers in Anansi's ear.)*

Anansi: You are right! I know just what to do.

Storyteller 2: So Anansi went and dug a big hole. He covered it with sticks. Soon Leopard came along. When Leopard walked across the sticks, he fell into the hole. What do you think Anansi will do now?

Anansi: Leopard, what are you doing in the hole?

Osebo: I don't know! I was prowling around last night, and I fell in this pit. I cannot get out. Will you help me?

Anansi: Of course I will help you. Give me your paws.

Storyteller 3: When Leopard reached up, Anansi grabbed his paws. Anansi quickly wrapped his thread around Osebo's paws. He wound it around and around. Then he took Leopard to Nyame.

Nyame: Anansi, have you brought me Osebo?

Anansi: Yes, I have brought you the leopard whose teeth are as sharp as spears.

Nyame: Very good, Anansi. Now you must bring me the hornet whose sting hurts like fire.

Storyteller 1: Now, Anansi was only a little spider. How could he capture such a fierce insect? Anansi let out his thread and dropped back to Earth. He went to his wife. Listen carefully to hear what happened.

Aso: How will you trap the hornet? Ah! I have an idea. Perhaps you could use this gourd. *(She whispers in Anansi's ear.)*

Storyteller 2: So Anansi went to the forest and found the hornets buzzing 'round their nest. Anansi poured water over the leaves on the ground and all over himself. The hornets buzzed toward him.

Mmoboro: What are you doing, Anansi?

Anansi: It is raining! Can't you feel it? I am hiding under this leaf. Quickly, it is dry inside this gourd. Fly in here!

Mmoboro: Thank you, Anansi. You are right! It is dry in here. The raindrops will not drown us now. Thank you! Buzzzzzz.

Storyteller 3: As soon as the hornets were inside the gourd, Anansi spun a tight web over the opening. The hornets were trapped. Anansi took them to Nyame.

Nyame: Anansi, I see you have brought me the hornet whose sting hurts like fire. You are very clever. But you will never catch the Wee One.

Anansi: I have a plan. I will return soon.

Storyteller 1: Anansi went home and spoke with Aso. Soon she made him a rag doll. Anansi spread sticky tree sap all over the doll. Then he went to where the Wee One plays. He placed the doll under the tree. Then Anansi attached his thread to the doll's head. He put yummy yams in the doll's lap. He hid in the tree.

Wee One: What is this? Yummy! Some yams. May I have some of your yams?

Storyteller 2: Anansi pulled the thread attached to the doll's head. It made the head nod "yes."

Wee One: *(eating the yams)* Thank you! May I have another? *(pause)* I said, May I have another? *(angry)* Why won't you answer me? You are very rude!

Storyteller 3: Upset, the Wee One grabbed the doll to shake her.

Wee One: Help! Help! My hand is stuck!

Storyteller 1: Anansi quickly wrapped up the Wee One in his thread. He took the Wee One to the sky god.

Nyame: Anansi, you have brought the Wee One. No one has ever seen a Wee One. How did you do it?

Anansi: I am very clever. I have paid your price. Now, Nyame, may I please have your stories to share?

Nyame: You have paid my price. I will give you the stories. From now on they will be called Spider Stories.

Storyteller 2: And so Anansi took the stories to the creatures of Earth. Now YOU must take this story and pass it on to someone else. Then it will come back to you.

Name _____

Trickster Questions

Mark the best answer for each question.

1. What did Anansi want from the sky god?
   ○ a snake   ○ a web   ○ stories   ○ a hornet

2. What did Anansi use to capture the python?
   ○ a palm branch ○ a large hole   ○ a gourd   ○ sticks

3. Who helped Anansi trick the animals?
   ○ the sky god   ○ his wife   ○ the python   ○ the leopard

4. What did Anansi use to tie up the leopard?
   ○ ropes   ○ tree vines   ○ string   ○ his thread

5. What did Nyame call the stories when he gave them to Anansi?
   ○ trickster tales ○ sky god stories ○ spider stories ○ yarns

Which character was the hardest to trick? Draw its picture here.

```



```

Name _____

Spider Math

Solve the problems below.

1. Anansi found a palm tree with 15 branches. He needed 4 branches to trap the python. How many branches were left on the tree after Anansi took what he needed?

   _____

2. Anansi dug a pit to catch the leopard. He dug the hole 4 feet deep. He decided it was not deep enough. He dug it 9 feet deeper. How many feet deep was the hole?

   _____

3. Anansi went to see the sky god 5 times. Each time he went he used 6 miles of thread. How much thread did he use in all?

   _____

4. Aso gave Anansi a gourd to use to catch the hornets. There were 27 hornets in all. All but 4 of the hornets flew into the gourd. How many hornets were inside the gourd?

   _____

5. Anansi needed sticks to cover the hole he dug. He went to one tree and took 8 sticks. He went to another tree and took 12 sticks. He went to the last tree and took 10 sticks. How many sticks did he have in all?

   _____

Now Presenting...

The Little Pollinators

Step into a fragrant garden and meet the creatures who are busy doing the sticky work of pollination.

12 parts

Setting the Stage

Background

Encourage students to speculate about why insects, birds, and other animals visit plants and flowers. If necessary, you may need to tell them that such visitors usually eat nectar or pollen from these plants. In doing so, they play a very important role in the pollination of plants—when pollen is carried from one plant to another on some part of their body.

Staging

Students may create simple headbands or necklaces featuring their own illustrations of the animals they represent in the performance. Provide images of bats, bees, butterflies, moths, and hummingbirds for students to examine before they create their illustrations. Or have children glue the pictures on page 88 to headbands or necklaces.

Encore

After performing this script, students may enjoy *The Magic School Bus Plants Seeds: A Book about How Living Things Grow* by Joanna Cole.

Vocabulary

Introduce and discuss the following words before reading the script:

nectar: a sweet liquid in flowers used by bees to make honey

pollen: a mass of dust-like grains produced by plants with seeds

protein: a material that is found in all cells; it is an important part of human and animal diets

twilight: a dim light in the sky just after sunset

Now Presenting...

The Little Pollinators

Insects and birds do important work when they travel from flower to flower. Each of these creatures is specially designed to do the important work of carrying pollen from one plant to another.

Characters

Chorus .... _____

_____

_____

Butterfly 1 .... _____

Butterfly 2 .... _____

Hummingbird 1 .... _____

Hummingbird 2 .... _____

Honeybee 1 .... _____

Honeybee 2 .... _____

Bumblebee .... _____

Moth .... _____

Bat .... _____

Readers' Theater, Grade 2 • EMC 3307

The Little Pollinators

······················ **Characters** ······················

Chorus   Honeybee 1
Butterfly 1   Honeybee 2
Butterfly 2   Bumblebee
Hummingbird 1   Moth
Hummingbird 2   Bat

Chorus: Springtime has come with sunshine bright.
Forests and gardens are a beautiful sight.
The birds and the bees are darting about,
spreading their magic as they fly in and out.
Springtime has come with sunshine bright.
It's a season of wonder and delight.

Butterfly 1: It's spring! I love spring! The flowers are blooming!
The sun is out! And it's so easy to find sweet nectar.

Butterfly 2: Did you see those blue flowers over there? I think I'll
flutter over and drink some of their yummy nectar.
Do you want to come along?

Butterfly 1: I smell something. Where is that sweet smell coming
from? Look at those pink and purple flowers. I am going
over there.

Butterfly 2: My tongue is ready for this meal.

Hummingbird 1: Excuse me! I think you're on my flower. I was just
about to take a sip here.

Butterfly 1: There are so many flowers around here. Why don't you try that red one over there? Those always have sweet nectar. My tongue is not long enough to drink from them. But it would be easy for you to get their nectar.

Hummingbird 1: You're right. I do love those red flowers. They are my favorite. And my beak can easily reach way down to the nectar. Thank you for pointing them out to me.

Hummingbird 2: What's that yellow dust all over your head? Are you going to a party?

Butterfly 1: No. I must have picked that up from the last flower I visited. Every time I go after that nectar, it gets all over my head and chest.

Hummingbird 1: That happens to me, too! I always seem to be covered in that powdery stuff from the flowers.

Butterfly 2: What are you two doing?

Hummingbird 1: We were just talking about all this powdery stuff we seem to get all over us when we drink from these flowers.

Butterfly 2: I've been told that it's really important stuff. It's called pollen. Certain flowers can't make seeds and fruit unless they have pollen from other flowers of the same type. If we didn't carry pollen from one plant to another, there would be no new plants!

Honeybee 1: You know what I call that yellow powdery stuff? FOOD! We honeybees love to eat that pollen. It is full of protein.

Honeybee 2: We even have special pouches on our legs called pollen baskets. We stuff them full of pollen to take back to the hive for the other bees. I LOVE pollen!

Bumblebee: I wish I had pollen baskets on my legs like you honeybees. Instead, my legs are covered with hair that the pollen sticks to.

Honeybee 1: And I wish I were as strong as you. I would love to taste the nectar in those yellow flowers over there. I'm not strong enough to get inside, and my tongue is too short to reach the nectar.

Butterfly 1: I would love to taste it, too, but there is nothing for me to land on. Is the nectar sweet and tasty?

Bumblebee: I must say, it is one of my favorites.

Hummingbird 1: I like the red flowers best. I think they have the sweetest nectar.

Honeybee 2: What is red?

Hummingbird 2: It's a color. It's bright and cheery. Red flowers are my favorites.

Bumblebee: We bees can't see the color that you call red. Red flowers just look dull to us. Our favorites are blue and purple.

Honeybee 2: And yellow!

Honeybee 1: It's getting dark. We need to head back to the hive.

Honeybee 2: I can't wait to tell the other bees what we've found. This is a bountiful garden. The other honeybees in the hive will enjoy it. Good night, everyone!

Hummingbird 1: I see a moth over on that white flower. It must be getting late if the moths are already arriving. I suppose it's time to go.

Moth: Good evening. This garden is beautiful. It smells so fragrant. That's why I decided to come over.

Hummingbird 2: You bees and moths are always talking about how wonderful everything smells. I wish I could smell things.

Hummingbird 1: I wish I could, too. It must be delightful. We hummingbirds cannot smell things like you.

Moth: Yes, enjoying a sweet scent certainly is a pleasure. I see this garden is full of beautiful white flowers. Is their nectar sweet?

Butterfly 1: Yes, it's just like sugar.

Butterfly 2: Moth, you must get very tired fluttering all the time. Why don't you ever land while you eat?

Moth: It would be nice to land on a flower petal while I eat, like you do. But it doesn't seem natural to me. I like to just flutter, flutter, flutter . . . just like the hummingbirds.

Bat: Good evening!

Butterflies 1 and 2: Stay away from us! Please don't eat us!

Bat: Oh, don't worry. I'm not that kind of bat. I like to eat the same things you do. I suck nectar from the flowers, too.

Moth: Thank goodness! Bats always make me nervous!

Bat: I see you have pollen stuck on your hair. It gets stuck on mine, too. I'll probably be totally dusted with it in a while.

Moth: Yes, I always seem to be covered with pollen. They say it helps the flowers. I've been told that each flower needs pollen from another flower of the same species in order to make seeds.

Bat: Yes, and without seeds, there would be no fruit! That would be terrible.

Hummingbird 1: Yes, just terrible. Well, it's twilight. It's time for us to go. Good-bye, Moth. Farewell, Bat. I hope you enjoy this wonderful garden tonight.

Hummingbird 2, Butterfly 1, Butterfly 2: Good night!

Moth: I hope you find sweet nectar tonight, Bat.

Bat: I hope so, too! Good evening.

Chorus: Springtime has come, the moon is bright.
Forests and gardens are a beautiful sight.
Moths and bats are darting about,
spreading their magic as they fly in and out.
Springtime has come, the moon is bright.
It's a season of wonder and delight.

Name _____

A Honeybee's Body

Write the name of each part of the honeybee's body on the correct line. Choose the words from the list below.

antenna	leg	head	eye
pollen basket	tongue	stinger	wing

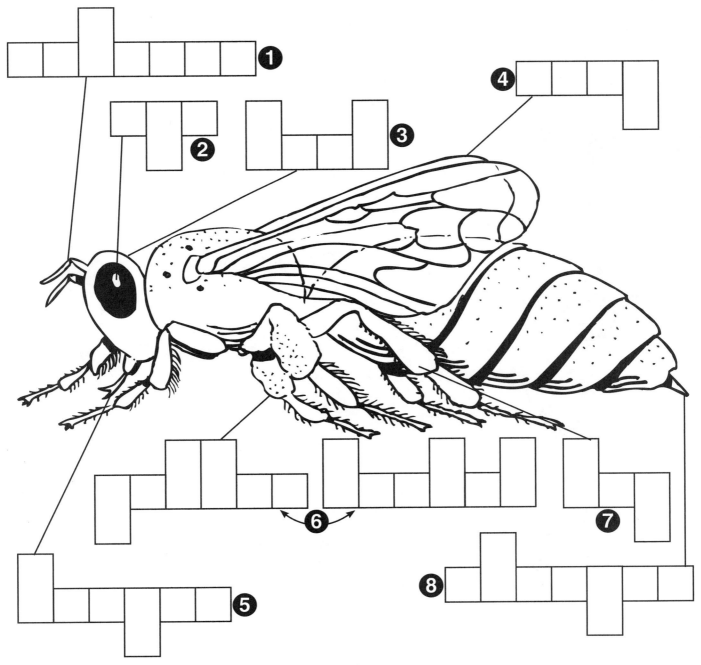

Readers' Theater, Grade 2 • EMC 3307

Name _____

Creatures' Features

Draw a line from each phrase to the creature it describes.
Some phrases can describe more than one creature.

flies at night

cannot smell

cannot see red

likes white flowers

carries pollen back for others

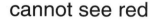

drinks nectar with a long tongue

does not land while drinking nectar

     Readers' Theater, Grade 2 • EMC 3307

George Washington Carver

George Washington Carver was a remarkable person. His never-ending search for knowledge helped him become a notable and widely respected scientist—an even more remarkable accomplishment for a man whose life began in slavery. He devoted his life to helping others better themselves. The roles in this script correspond to the letters in Carver's name, like an acrostic.

Setting the Stage

Background

George Washington Carver was born into slavery in Missouri in about 1865. After his mother died, he was raised on the farm of Moses and Susan Carver. Carver began his education at home, but the Carvers later sent him to a school for black children. He went on to graduate from Iowa State University, and later became the first African American faculty member there. His dream was to train African Americans so that they could find meaningful employment, and he pursued this through teaching. Some of his most noteworthy work in botany began as he sought ways to improve soil depleted by the cultivation of tobacco and cotton. He introduced the concept of crop rotation, using peanuts and sweet potatoes—plants that added much-needed nitrogen to the soil. Because people were unfamiliar with ways to use these plants, he worked to develop 325 products using peanuts and 108 using sweet potatoes.

As you share some of this information with students, you may wish to mention that some of the products he developed from peanuts included peanut butter, shampoo, dyes, face powder, and oil. Products made from the sweet potato included flour, starch, molasses, and ink.

Staging

If you have 23 readers, you may assign one student for each letter in Carver's name. Or have one student read several parts. Have students create placards with the letter that corresponds to their role on one side and their lines from the script on the other. Position students in the order they will read. After students read their lines, they may hold up their placards to spell out "GEORGE WASHINGTON CARVER."

Encore

You and your students may follow some of Dr. Carver's own simple recipes using peanuts! Check them out on this Iowa State University Web site (www.lib.iastate.edu/spcl/gwc/resources/furtherresearch.html).

Vocabulary

Introduce and discuss the following words before reading the script:

astonish: to fill with wonder, surprise, or amazement

crop: an agricultural product that is growing or is already harvested

extraordinary: way beyond the ordinary; very unusual or exceptional

genius: great and unique creative ability in art or science

mend: to sew up a tear

research: careful study and investigation that allows you to understand or discover facts

slave: a human being who is owned by another as property, has no rights, and is not free

soil: the surface layer of Earth; the dirt where plant life grows

whittle: to shape a small piece of wood by cutting it with a knife

Now Presenting...

George Washington Carver

George Washington Carver had a dream. He wanted to help his people become independent. He learned everything he could about plants and soil. He taught farmers how to grow new crops and create new products from them. He made his dream come true.

Characters

Narrator_____   Reader 12 (N): _____

Reader 1 (G): _____   Reader 13 (G): _____

Reader 2 (E): _____   Reader 14 (T): _____

Reader 3 (O): _____   Reader 15 (O): _____

Reader 4 (R): _____   Reader 16 (N): _____

Reader 5 (G): _____   Reader 17 (C): _____

Reader 6 (E): _____   Reader 18 (A): _____

Reader 7 (W): _____   Reader 19 (R): _____

Reader 8 (A): _____   Reader 20 (V): _____

Reader 9 (S): _____   Reader 21 (E): _____

Reader 10 (H): _____   Reader 22 (R): _____

Reader 11 (I): _____

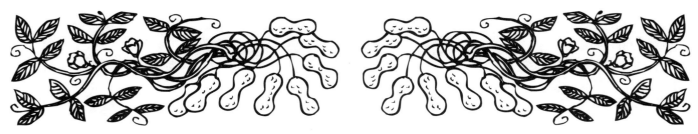

George Washington Carver

Narrator: George Washington Carver had a dream. He wanted to help poor farmers. He learned all he could about soil and crops. He taught farmers what to plant. He taught farmers that planting peanuts and sweet potatoes would enrich the soil. He taught people how to help themselves. He made his dream come true!

Reader 1 (G): G is for "George Washington Carver." He was a man with a dream. He loved plants. He wanted to help farmers grow better crops.

Reader 2 (E): E is for "extraordinary." George was an extraordinary person. He wanted to learn about everything. He never gave up. He became a good artist and a famous scientist.

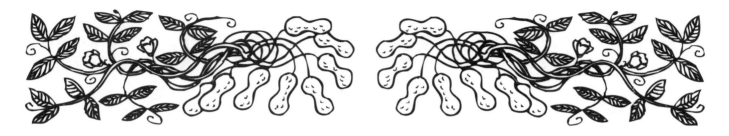

Reader 3 (O): O is for "owned." When George was born, his mother was a slave. She was owned by Moses and Susan Carver. George wasn't sure when he was born, but he believed it was in 1865.

Reader 4 (R): R is for "rescued." When George was just a baby, he and his mother were kidnapped by slave raiders. Baby George was rescued and returned to the home of Moses and Susan Carver. They cared for him and raised him.

Reader 5 (G): G is for "genius." George was a genius with plants. Even as a boy, he loved plants and insects. In fact, people were already calling him "the plant doctor" when he was still a child! He made the Carver's garden the most beautiful in town.

Reader 6 (E): E is for "everything." That's what George wanted to know about: everything! He wanted to learn and learn and learn! He left the Carver's home when he was 12 years old. He went to live in another town where there was a school he could attend. At night, he slept in a barn.

Reader 7 (W): W is for "work." George worked hard for the families he lived with. He cooked and washed and mended clothes. He was not very strong. Even his voice was small and squeaky, but he always worked hard! He had to earn money to pay for school.

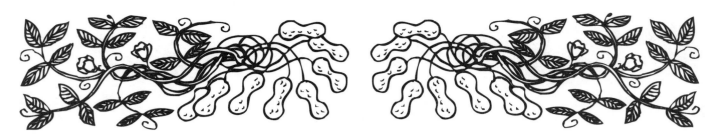

Reader 8 (A): A is for "Aunt Mariah," the lady who gave George a place to live while he went to school. He had to help Aunt Mariah do laundry. He studied while he did the wash. When George was 13, he had to find a new school. He had learned everything his first school could teach him. He left Aunt Mariah's house. He went to another town with a better school.

Reader 9 (S): S is for "science." George knew a lot about science. In his new school, he even taught the teacher new things! George started a laundry business when he was 13. He washed clothes as a way to earn money to pay for his new school.

Reader 10 (H): H is for "hardworking." George worked very hard all the time. He worked hard to earn money for school. He worked hard in school. When he wasn't working hard, he loved to draw and to whittle wood. He was a wonderful artist.

Reader 11 (I): I is for "I can do that!" That was what George believed, and that was how he acted. Even though George was weak and small, he always tried to do new things. He always said, "I can do that!"

Reader 12 (N): N is for "never give up." George had a dream of going to college. He moved from city to city. He washed lots of clothes to earn money. When he finished high school, he began looking for a college that would accept black students.

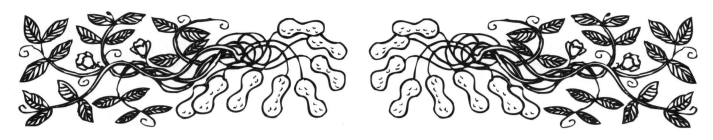

Reader 13 (G): G is for "graduate." George finally found a college in Iowa. He studied agriculture. He studied plants and learned about growing crops. He learned how plants grow best. He graduated from college when he was 30 years old.

Reader 14 (T): T is for "teacher." When George finished college, he became a teacher. He taught other students about plants. The students liked George. He was an interesting teacher.

Reader 15 (O): O is for "opportunity." George had a dream. He wanted to help poor black farmers grow better crops. A man named Booker T. Washington asked George to come teach in Alabama. He wanted George to teach poor farmers how to grow healthy plants.

Reader 16 (N): N is for "new." Everything was new for George when he went to Alabama. He taught at the Tuskegee Institute. George grew plants with his students. They learned about the soil. George loved his new home.

Reader 17 (C): C is for "crop rotation." Most farmers were used to planting just one crop: cotton. As time went by, the soil became unhealthy. Farmers could hardly grow anything. George taught farmers how to make the soil healthy again. They would plant cotton one year, and peanuts or sweet potatoes the next year. This is called crop rotation. It kept the soil strong and healthy.

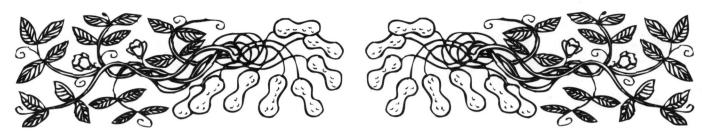

Reader 18 (A): A is for "astonish." People were astonished when George told them to plant peanuts and sweet potatoes. They said that no one would buy peanuts.

Reader 19 (R): R is for "research." George did research. He found ways to use peanuts and sweet potatoes. George discovered hundreds of ways to use these products. People started buying peanuts and sweet potatoes.

Reader 20 (V): V is for "valuable." George taught his students valuable lessons. They earned more money when they sold their crops. They learned how to be good farmers.

Reader 21 (E): E is for "experiments." George used experiments as a way to teach people how to improve their farming. He built a wagon to carry his experiments and tools. George showed his experiments to farmers. They learned a lot from George.

Reader 22 (R): R is for "remarkable." George Washington Carver was a remarkable man. He was called the "Wizard of Tuskegee." He earned many awards for his hard work. He made his dream come true! He helped his people.

Everyone: Thank you, George Washington Carver!

Name _____

Peanut Products

George Washington Carver made all of these products using peanuts. Now, list them in alphabetical order. The first one has been done for you.

ink   *candy* _____

soap   _____

oil   _____

flour   _____

paint   _____

dyes   _____

rubber   _____

candy   _____

glue   _____

lotion   _____

Name _____

The Peanut Plant

The peanut plant first grew in South America. It grows to be about 18 inches tall and 36 inches across. Each plant produces from 25 to 50 peanuts.

Look at this diagram of a peanut plant. Use the words at the bottom of the page to label each part. Then color the picture.

| leaf | peanut | peg | yellow flower |
| soil level | stem | roots | |

Now Presenting...

The Giant Squash and the Erie Canal

This tall tale about a farmer's efforts to keep an enormous squash plant healthy is set along New York's Erie Canal—one of the first great civil engineering projects to capture the American imagination.

Setting the Stage

Background

Use a map to point out to students the location of Lake Erie and the Hudson River, and the Appalachian Mountains separating them. Explain that in 1825, the Erie Canal was dug to help create an uninterrupted water route for the transportation of goods throughout the state of New York. It extended a canal system that had been established by the state government of New York in 1792. The Erie Canal helped develop commerce and opened up New York State for settlement and farming.

The Erie Canal stretched across the state of New York from Buffalo to the Hudson River. The canal was originally 40 feet wide at the top and 4 feet deep. Mules walked along a towpath that ran alongside the canal, towing flat-bottomed barges laden with goods. The construction of the Erie Canal was one of the first major works of civil engineering in the United States, and it quickly captured the public's imagination. Over time, stories about the canal grew into tall tales. This script recounts one of them.

Staging

You may wish to use a gourd or even a rock to represent the seed, and green yarn for the growing vine.

Encore

Students may enjoy learning more about the Erie Canal by reading *The Erie Canal* by Peter Spier and *The Amazing, Impossible Erie Canal* by Cheryl Harness.

Vocabulary

Introduce and discuss the following words before reading the script:

barge: a large, flat-bottomed boat used for carrying cargo on a canal

canal: a waterway created by people for transporting goods

hoggee: (HOE-gee) the person who drives the mules along the towpath

shrivel: to shrink or become wrinkled and withered

squash: a plant with a vine that produces a vegetable

tow: to pull

towpath: the area alongside a canal where mules walk as they pull a barge

The Giant Squash and the Erie Canal

A farmer who lives along the Erie Canal is trying to keep a special squash plant healthy. During a spell of dry weather, he is prepared to try just about anything to water his extraordinary plant.

Characters

Narrator .... _____

Farmer .... _____

Farmer's Wife............................ _____

Farmer's Daughter .... _____

Farmer's Son .... _____

Neighbor .... _____

Hoggee .... _____

Hoggee's Wife........................... _____

Hoggee's Daughter .... _____

Hoggee's Son .... _____

The Giant Squash
and the Erie Canal

························ **Characters** ························

Narrator   Neighbor
Farmer   Hoggee
Farmer's Wife   Hoggee's Wife
Farmer's Daughter   Hoggee's Daughter
Farmer's Son   Hoggee's Son

Narrator: When I was up in New York State, I heard a story. It was about a GIANT squash. I mean a squash as big as a truck. They say this really happened around the year 1833. Here's how the story goes. When it's over, you can tell me if you believe it or not.

Farmer's Wife: What do you have there, Jed?

Farmer: I found this thing on the towpath. I thought it was a rock. But it sure looks like a seed to me.

Farmer's Daughter: That can't be a seed, Pa! It's as big as a watermelon.

Farmer's Son: It must have fallen off a barge, though I can't imagine how the hoggee didn't notice—it's enormous!

Farmer: I think I'll plant it and see what happens. Son, you're going to have to go to the canal and fill some buckets with water. It hasn't rained in so long that our well has gone dry. If this really is a seed, it will no doubt need a lot of water!

Farmer's Son: Oh Pa! Those buckets are so heavy!

Farmer: Well, if that rain would only come, you wouldn't have to carry water. So start wishing for rain.

Narrator: So the farmer's son carried five buckets of water from the canal every day. Still no rain came. So he carried some more.

Neighbor: My gosh, Ned, that rock you stuck in the ground seems to be growing. In fact, it seems to be growing pretty fast.

Farmer: Yep! It really was a seed! Why just yesterday we saw a little green sprout popping up. Today there is a 10-foot vine! But it had better rain pretty soon. That vine will shrivel up and die if we don't get some rain. My son is sure getting tired of carrying those buckets of water from the canal.

Farmer's Wife: Well, Jed, I don't see any clouds up in that blue sky.

Narrator: And so it went. Day after day, there was no rain, no clouds, and clear blue skies. Until one day . . .

Farmer's Son: Pa! Pa! A hoggee saw me taking water out of the canal today. He said if he catches me taking more water, I won't see the sunshine tomorrow.

Farmer: But we must water our plant! We've got to find a way! That plant is amazing! It's the biggest thing I've ever seen!

Narrator: So the farmer thought and thought. Then he thought some more. After he had thought for a long, long time, he had an idea.

Farmer: Come on, everybody! It's time to water our plant. Make a circle. Okay, are you all ready? Spit! Ready? Spit! Ready? Spit! Spit! Spit!

Narrator: The farmer's family spit on that old plant all day and all night for two days.

Farmer's Daughter: Pa, I can't do this any more.

Farmer's Son: Yeah Pa, I ran out of spit yesterday.

Farmer's Wife: Ned, the children are right.

Narrator: So that farmer started thinking again. After a while he jumped up and down and started dancing around.

Farmer: Okay, everybody! Quit spittin'. I have an idea!

Narrator: Later that night . . .

Farmer: Shhhh! I'm almost done digging this thing up. Now use those ropes to tie the plant to the horses and we'll drag it. Be careful, now!

Farmer's Daughter: Where are we going, Pa?

Farmer: We're going down to the canal. We're going to plant the squash next to the canal. Then its roots can get water right from the canal.

Farmer's Son: Pa sure is smart, isn't he? I wonder how big this here plant will get? It's already 200 feet long!

Narrator: So the farmer and his family planted that squash plant right next to the Erie Canal. Then they went home and went to bed. The next day . . .

Farmer: Hurry! Hurry! Let's go down and look at our plant! I hope it didn't die during the night.

Farmer's Son: WOW! That was a smart thing to do, Pa. It looks like that plant grew another hundred feet last night.

 Readers' Theater, Grade 2 • EMC 3307

Narrator: The family was so busy admiring their plant that they didn't notice a barge stuck nearby in the canal. Much as the hoggee prodded and pleaded, his mules could not budge the barge.

Hoggee: The canal has just dried up! We're stuck. The mules can't move us another inch.

Hoggee's Son: Da, Da, it's the same all up and down the canal. I just ran way down the towpath, and there are barges stopped for as far as I can see. The water is all gone!

Hoggee's Wife: What is that green up ahead? It looks like a mountain! It looks like a mountain of vines.

Hoggee's Son and Daughter: We'll run up and see what it is.

Hoggee's Wife: Now be careful!

Hoggee's Son and Daughter: What is it?

Hoggee's Daughter: It looks like a plant. And there is a huge yellow thing growing on it! It's bigger than our boat. It looks like a squash.

Farmer's Daughter: That's our plant! My Pa planted it. It grew 100 feet last night.

Hoggee: Well, it looks like that plant sucked all the water out of the Erie Canal. There is no water left! Our barges are all stuck.

Farmer's Wife: Look! Look! Look at those clouds over there! It appears it is finally going to rain. Soon you'll have enough water to pull your barge!

Hoggee: It had better rain. We have to get this wheat to New York harbor soon!

Narrator: The next day it did rain. It rained so hard it filled the Erie Canal right back up. The barges were able to move on. Many went to New York harbor. Others went toward Buffalo. Horses and mules towed them all. A month later, the hoggee and his family were once again guiding their barge past the farmer's land.

Hoggee's Wife: Well, I'll be! Look at that. Looks like they made a store out of that ol' squash.

Hoggee's Son: What are they selling?

Hoggee's Daughter: Let's go see.

Farmer: Welcome back! Would you like to buy a length of strong green hose?

Farmer's Daughter: We used the veins from our squash vines to make hoses. They're strong and they're long. And, boy, can they ever carry water!

Hoggee: You'd better keep it yourself. Next time you plant squash, you can use that hose to get water from Lake Erie. Then the canal won't run dry.

Farmer: Good idea! Because you can bet your bottom dollar that we saved the seeds from our squash to plant come springtime!

Narrator: Now, you tell me what you think. Did this really happen, or is it just a whopping tall tale?

Squash Math

Solve the problems below. Show your answers in pictures, too.

1. The squash plant grew 10 feet a day. How many feet will it grow in 10 days? _____	2. The farmer's son gave the squash 5 buckets of water each day. How many buckets of water did he give the plant in 6 days? _____
3. The farmer's family used the squash vine to make hoses. Each hose was 23 feet long. How long would 3 hoses be? _____	4. Each barge is towed through the canal by 2 mules. How many mules would you need to pull 12 canal boats? _____

Name _____

Check Your Memory

Write a complete sentence to answer each question. Reread the script to check your answers.

1. Where did the squash seed come from?

   _____

   _____

2. How was the squash seed watered in the beginning?

   _____

   _____

3. Why couldn't the family water the seed with well water?

   _____

   _____

4. How did the family water the plant after the hoggee asked them not to use canal water?

   _____

   _____

5. About how much did the vine grow each night?

   _____

   _____

6. Why did the canal dry up?

   _____

   _____

7. What would you do if you had a squash plant that was 500 feet long?

   _____

   _____

 Readers' Theater, Grade 2 • EMC 3307

Now Presenting...

Lion Dancer

Lee wants to participate in the Lion Dance in the Chinese New Year parade, but he doesn't want to miss out on other activities in order to practice. Can he make his family proud without giving up the things he enjoys?

Setting the Stage

Background

In the Chinese culture, the lion is a symbol of power, wisdom, and good fortune. The Lion Dance is performed during Chinese New Year celebrations and other special occasions. The dancers train many long hours in the martial art of kung fu. The Lion Dancers bring honor to their families by performing this dance.

Chinese New Year usually comes in February, and includes many special traditions. It is a time for families to be together and to remember and honor their ancestors. Special foods that are considered lucky are prepared and eaten. Children receive "lucky money" in special red envelopes. People with Chinese heritage who live in the United States and other countries outside of China continue to maintain many of these traditions.

Staging

The lion may wear the mask made in the activity on pages 114 and 115. If the mask is mounted on a stick, the reader can move it away from his or her face while speaking.

Encore

Read the book *Lion Dancer* by Kate Waters. You might contact a local kung fu organization and invite them to present a demonstration of the Lion Dance to your class.

Vocabulary

Introduce and discuss the following words before reading the script:

ancestor: a person in your family who lived before you were born

China: a country in Asia

emperor: the ruler of an empire; similar to a king who rules a kingdom

honor: great respect that is given or received

kung fu: a Chinese system of self-defense

native: belonging to or coming from a particular country

reluctant: unwilling to do something

Lion Dancer

Lee wants to participate in the Lion Dance for this year's Chinese New Year's celebration. But he must first decide which is more important to him: practicing for the Lion Dance or having fun.

Characters

Lion .... _____

Lee .... _____
(an 8-year-old Chinese-American boy)

Jenny (Lee's sister) .... _____

Dad (Lee's father) .... _____

Mom (Lee's mother) .... _____

Master Liu .... _____
(Lee's kung fu teacher)

Michael..................................... _____

Chen .... _____

Lion Dancer

························· **Characters** ·······················

Lion	Mom
Lee	Master Liu
Jenny	Michael
Dad	Chen

Lion: Good day! I am the famous lion of China. I bring good fortune and happiness to people. Lions are not native to China. Hundreds of years ago, travelers brought lions from other areas as gifts to the emperors. The Lion Dance has been performed since that time. I am here to help tell the story of Lee, a boy who is learning to be a lion dancer in a Chinese New Year's celebration.

Jenny: The New Year is almost here. I'm getting so excited! I can't wait to put on my new clothes and open the red "lucky money" envelopes from all the relatives.

Lee: And I can't wait to wear my lion costume and dance in the parade tomorrow.

Jenny: Mom says you will bring our family honor by dancing in the parade and doing your best. I wish I could dance, too.

Lee: You might not feel the same if you had to go to practice.

Jenny: You really do have to practice a lot. It seems like that's all you do in your free time these days.

Lee: Well, kung fu training takes lots of time. Yesterday, Paul placed third in the skating finals over at the skate park. I know I could've done just as well, but I had to go to practice.

Jenny: I'm not sure I could give up a chance to be in a contest like that. I guess you'd rather bring honor to our family than just win a ribbon for yourself.

Lee: I'm not really sure that's what I want. I do know one thing, though. If I can save up for new skates, I will definitely enter the skating contest next month.

Jenny: How much are the new skates?

Lee: I want the latest in-line skates, and they cost about $65.00. I already have $20.00.

Jenny: Maybe you'll get enough "lucky money" to buy them.

Lee: Maybe . . .

Dad: Lee, you'd better get ready to go to practice. Mom already packed a snack and some lunch for you. I bet Master Liu will have you three lion dancers practicing all day long to be sure you're ready for the Lion Dance tomorrow.

Lee: But Dad, I was planning on going over to the skate park with Paul for a few hours.

Dad: I know, but this is such an important honor for our family. Don't you want to do a good job, especially since Master Liu has given you the honor of working the lion's head? I know this isn't an easy choice, Lee. But how will the other two lion dancers feel if the lion's head is out of step?

Lee: I guess you're right . . . I just don't want to miss out on the skating contest.

Mom: Lee, Dad and I promise you can sign up for next month's contest. After the New Year's parade is over, you'll have lots more time to practice your skating.

Lee: I guess you're right. I'll call Paul to tell him I can't go.

Jenny: Well, I'm going on a bike ride with Anna. Good luck, Lee.

Dad: I'll take you over to your practice, Lee. Let me know when you're ready.

Lion: So Lee reluctantly went off to his kung fu practice. Even though he worked hard to master the steps of the Lion Dance, he couldn't stop thinking about the skating contest he was missing.

Master Liu: Lee, I'm so glad you're here. Today you need to practice pulling the cords in the lion's head. The one on the left makes the ears wiggle. The other cord makes the eyes blink. And the switch behind the nose will make the lights go on. You have a lot of responsibility. Are you sure you want to do this?

Lee: Yes, Master Liu. I am ready.

Michael: I'm ready to be in the tail. Where is Chen? He needs to be here to practice teasing the lion with his fan.

Chen: Here I am! I'm ready to tease the lion. Here's my fan.

Master Liu: Remember boys, the lion must always be moving and never in a straight line!

Michael: I've practiced. I'll be holding my end up! Get it?

Lee: Very funny! I don't think I'll stop moving my feet for a moment when I've got firecrackers going off all around me!

Lion: Lee, Michael, and Chen practiced with Master Liu for the rest of the day. They were very tired by the time they finally got home.

Mom: I'm glad you're home. I have prepared special dishes for our New Year's dinner. Go wash up.

Dad: And put on your new clothes. I'm just finishing up here with our family altar to honor our ancestors.

Lion: Lee's family had a wonderful New Year's dinner. Lee could hardly get to sleep that night as he went over and over the steps for the Lion Dance in his mind. Before he knew it, New Year's Day had come. His parents dropped him off at Master Liu's before they went with Jenny to find a spot to watch the parade.

Master Liu: Boys, put your costumes on and get ready for the parade.

Michael: I'm a little nervous about the firecrackers. Are you scared?

Lee: I am a little, but it will be all right. We are Lion Dancers!

Lion: The New Year's parade was wonderful. The Lion Dancers danced through the streets. Lee and the other boys remembered all their martial arts steps. A huge brightly colored dragon with 25 people under it danced behind them. The streets were covered with red paper from the firecrackers. The people of Chinatown threw many red envelopes at the dancers.

Dad: You did a wonderful job, Lee! You remembered all the steps. You made the ears and eyes move the whole time. The people loved the bright lights in the mask. You were a great lion dancer!

Lee: It was fun! I was so excited! But my ears are still ringing from all the noisy firecrackers.

Jenny: Lee, Lee! Did you get enough money to buy your skates?

Lee: I don't know. Will you help me open my envelopes and count the money?

Jenny: Sure!

Mom: Lee, you have honored our family. It was hard work. I know it was hard to give up your skating in order to practice. I hope you feel that you made the right choice.

Lee: It did take a lot of time, but I'm glad I chose to practice instead of going skating. I can go skating any day—but I can only be in the Lion Dance on special days.

Dad: We're proud of you, Lee!

Jenny: I've counted $15, Lee.

Lee: And I've counted $20. With the money I already have and the allowance money I'll get by next month, I think I'll have enough to buy new skates for the contest! You know something? I have a feeling this is going to be a great new year!

Name _____

Make a Lion Mask

The Lion Dance is performed during Chinese New Year. The lion brings good luck and scares away evil spirits. Follow these directions to make your own lion mask.

Materials
- 1 white 9" (23 cm) paper plate
- 15 1" x 6" (2.5 x 15 cm) yellow construction paper strips for the mane
- 10 cotton balls for the beard
- page 115, reproduced for each student
- 1 craft stick
- glue
- scissors
- crayons or other materials to decorate your mask (such as paint, sequins, pipe cleaners, yarn, feathers, or glitter)

Steps to Follow

1. Hold the plate over your face and have a partner help you mark the place to glue the eyes (right over your eyes).

2. Color and cut out the four pattern pieces.

3. Glue the pattern pieces onto the plate. Be sure to glue the eyes over the places marked on your plate.

4. Decorate the mask with crayons or other materials.

5. Curl the yellow strips by wrapping them around a pencil. Glue them to the outside edge of the paper plate to make the mane.

6. Glue on the cotton balls to make the lion's beard.

7. Attach the craft stick to the bottom of the mask.

8. Have your teacher help you make holes in the eyes so you can see.

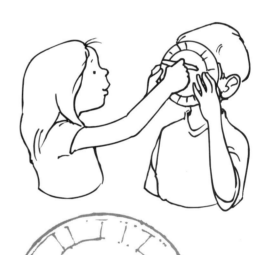

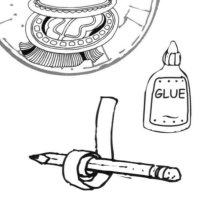

Lion Mask Pattern Pieces

 Readers' Theater, Grade 2 • EMC 3307

Now Presenting...

How Beetle Got Her Jeweled Coat

This story explains how a plain brown beetle from the Brazilian rainforest came to have beautiful, jewel-like colors.

Setting the Stage

Background

"How Beetle Got Her Jeweled Coat" is a *pourquoi* tale (from the French word for "why"). These tales explain how things in nature came to be the way they are today. Before reading the script, you may wish to point out Brazil on a map, and show children the large expanse of Amazonia, the largest rainforest on Earth. Children may be interested to learn that although tropical forests take up less than 7 percent of Earth's surface, more than half of all the planet's plant and animal species are found there.

Invite children to mention animals that are found in rainforests, and introduce any of the animal characters that are unfamiliar to them, such as the sloth, the jaguarundi (a member of the cat family that grows to about 26 inches in length and is an excellent swimmer), or the capybara (the largest member of the rodent family with a weight of about 100 pounds and a length of 4 feet, similar in appearance to a guinea pig, and fond of water). You may also wish to mention that many precious gemstones are found in Brazil, and that Brazil's flag is yellow and green.

Staging

Have the readers sit together at one side of the stage area. Another student may hold a simple palm tree prop at the other side of the stage. As the action shifts to the palm tree at the end of the race, readers could move to that area. To create a simple palm tree, tape together several cardboard wrapping paper tubes and cover them with brown butcher paper; stuff palm fronds cut from green butcher paper into the top tube.

Encore

After reading the script, you may wish to compare the plot to Aesop's classic fable *The Tortoise and the Hare,* using a Venn diagram. Or compare it to another pourquoi tale, such as Verna Aardema's *Why Mosquitoes Buzz in People's Ears.*

Vocabulary

Introduce and discuss the following words before reading the script:

accomplishment: something that has been done successfully

cliff: a high, steep rock face

emerald: a very valuable and beautiful green gemstone found in Brazil

palm: a tall tropical tree with a long, bare trunk and large leaves shaped like feathers at the top

topaz: a valuable yellow gemstone found in Brazil

How Beetle Got Her Jeweled Coat

Can Beetle win a race against Capybara? If she wins, her prize will be a coat of jewel-like colors instead of her dreary brown shell.

Characters

Narrator 1 .... _____

Narrator 2 .... _____

Narrator 3 .... _____

Capybara .... _____

Monkey .... _____

Jaguarundi .... _____

Beetle .... _____

Parrot .... _____

How Beetle Got Her Jeweled Coat

·················· **Characters** ··················

Narrator 1   Monkey
Narrator 2   Jaguarundi
Narrator 3   Beetle
Capybara   Parrot

Narrator 1: In Brazil's Amazon jungle on the continent of South America lives the beautifully colored Brazilian beetle. Her brilliant coat of bright yellow and green shimmers like a jewel in the sunlight.

Narrator 2: But the Brazilian beetle wasn't always so beautiful. Hundreds of years ago, Beetle had a plain, ordinary brown coat.

Narrator 3: This tale tells how a beetle of long ago earned the beautiful jeweled coat worn today by all Brazilian beetles.

Narrator 1: It happened on a bright and sunny day. Many of the animals were resting in the afternoon sunshine. A little beetle was crawling along when she happened upon a huge capybara.

Capybara: Beetle, you certainly do crawl slowly. You will never get anywhere in this world.

Monkey: You are right, Capybara. Beetle truly is a slow one. I have been sitting here for an hour and she has only crawled inches.

Capybara: Watch me! I can run fast, fast, fast! Watch me run to the water and back.

Monkey: Capybara can run fast, Beetle. Watch him carefully.

Jaguarundi: Capybara must run fast, or I will catch him! He would be a tasty dinner for me. I will keep my eye on him.

Narrator 2: Capybara ran to the water. He even jumped in for a quick splash. Then he came out, shook off, turned around, and ran back to Beetle. Sure enough, she had only crawled one inch along the path.

Capybara: Don't you wish that you could run like I do? Did you see how fast I am? I can run faster than almost anything in the jungle. I am a great runner!

Beetle: You surely are a very great runner. I think you are the fastest runner I have ever seen.

Narrator 3: Beetle was very polite. Her mother had taught her never to boast about her accomplishments. She quietly started to crawl on.

Parrot: I have heard that you think you are a great runner, Capybara.

Capybara: Yes, I am a very fast runner. I can probably run faster than you can fly.

Parrot: Well, I'm not sure about that. Since you think you are so fast, why don't you race against Beetle? Do you think you can beat her to that palm tree at the top of the cliff?

Capybara: Of course I can! I am a great runner! I am the best runner in the jungle. I can beat anyone who comes my way.

Jaguarundi: I'm not sure about that, Capybara!

Parrot: Let us have a race. Capybara shall race Beetle to the palm tree by the cliff. I will offer a prize to the winner of the race. The winner of the race shall have a beautiful new coat, specially made to order.

Capybara: I can tell you what kind of a coat I want right now. I am tired of my dull, brown coat. I love the bright yellow and brown coat of the jungle cat. I think it will look very handsome on my back. You can begin to make my new coat now, Parrot.

Beetle: I, too, would like a new coat. Capybara is right—a plain brown coat is dull and tiresome. I would like to have a coat as brightly colored as sparkling jewels.

Capybara: So, you think you can beat me, Beetle? You are slower than a turtle! You are almost as slow as the sloth hanging in the tree. You will never win the new coat!

Jaguarundi: Capybara, be careful with your bragging.

Parrot: I am ready to give the signal for the race to start. Are you ready, Beetle? Are you ready, Capybara?

Beetle: I am ready.

Capybara: Of course I am ready! This will be easy. I can't wait to see the beautiful coat that will be made for me.

Monkey: They both look ready to me, Parrot! I'll swing on ahead to see who wins.

Jaguarundi: *(quietly)* I will go to the palm tree on the cliff to wait for Capybara. Yum!

Parrot: Get ready! Get set! Go!

Narrator 1: And so little Beetle started walking slowly toward the palm tree far up on the cliff.

Narrator 2: Capybara, too, headed toward the palm tree far up on the cliff, running just as fast as he could.

Narrator 3: Parrot flew up to the palm tree on the cliff so he could see who arrived first. Monkey and Jaguarundi followed close behind Capybara.

Monkey: Capybara, you are almost halfway to the palm tree on the cliff. I can't even see Beetle. She must be far behind.

Capybara: That silly Beetle! She is foolish to think she can beat me. I am getting a little tired, though. Why should I hurry when I know I can beat that slow little beetle? I think I will walk for a while.

Monkey: Capybara, my friend, you should keep running! This is a race! You do not want to lose!

Jaguarundi: Show us, Capybara. Show us how fast you can run.

Capybara: All right. I will run. You are right—this is a race, and I am going to win.

Narrator 1: Capybara ran. Finally, he came to the palm tree at the top of the cliff. When he stopped to catch his breath, he was shocked to see Beetle already there, waiting for him alongside Parrot.

Capybara: Beetle, how did you ever get here before me? I can run faster than you! How did you do it? You must have cheated!

Beetle: I did not cheat. I flew.

Capybara: I did not know you could fly.

Parrot: You are foolish, Capybara. You should never judge anyone by looks alone. You can never tell who has wings hidden beneath their plain brown coat.

Jaguarundi: You have lost the race, Capybara! Beetle has won!

Parrot: What color do you wish your coat to be, little Beetle?

Narrator 2: Little Beetle looked at Parrot's beautiful yellow and green feathers. She looked at the green and gold palm tree above their heads. She saw the golden sun shining on the green jungle and hills.

Beetle: I will choose a coat that is the yellow of the shimmering sun and the green of the palm tree above.

Parrot: Then we shall make you a shiny coat of yellow and green. It will sparkle like green emeralds and glitter like yellow topaz.

Narrator 3: And that is how Brazilian beetles came to have the beautiful jeweled coats they wear today. And what happened to Capybara? Ask Jaguarundi!

Name _____

Real and Make-Believe

Read these sentences about the animals in the script. If the
information in the sentence is true, write a **T** by the sentence.
If the information is make-believe, write an **M**.

1. _____ Beetles and capybaras live in the Amazon Rainforest.

2. _____ Beetles and capybaras like to have races.

3. _____ Rainforest animals wear special coats.

4. _____ Capybaras like to swim.

5. _____ Beetles can crawl and fly.

6. _____ Parrots are fast swimmers.

7. _____ Monkeys can swing through the treetops.

8. _____ Capybaras have bright, colorful fur.

9. _____ Capybaras like to eat jaguarundis.

10. _____ It's not a good idea to judge others by looks alone.

In Your Opinion

Write about how Beetle won the race. Did she trick Capybara? Explain your answer.

_____

_____

_____

_____

_____

_____

_____

_____

_____

_____

Now Presenting...

The Lost Kitten

Stephanie and Reid find a little kitten and take it home. When they find out someone has lost a kitten in their neighborhood, they must decide what to do. What choice will Stephanie and Reid make?

Setting the Stage

Background

Making difficult decisions is something all children face. This script gives the class a chance to discuss the decision Stephanie and Reid have to make. The first time you read through the script, you may wish to pause on page 130 and invite students to share their ideas about the right thing to do.

Encore

To continue exploring the issues related to character development and honesty, read *A Day's Work* by Eve Bunting, *The Talking Eggs* by R. San Souci, or *Big Fat Enormous Lie* by Marjorie Weinman Sharmat.

Vocabulary

Introduce and discuss the following word before reading the script:

heartbreaking: something that is very sad or disappointing

Now Presenting...

The Lost Kitten

Stephanie and Reid have found a kitten. They love the kitten and take good care of it. But does the kitten really belong to them?

Characters

Narrator..................................... _____

Reid.. _____

Stephanie.................................. _____

Mom .... _____

Dad .... _____

Mr. Khan (pet-store owner) .... _____

Uriel.. _____

Nicole .... _____

The Lost Kitten

Characters

Narrator	Dad
Reid	Mr. Khan
Stephanie	Uriel
Mom	Nicole

Narrator: Reid and Stephanie, 8-year-old twins, are hanging around the house on a Saturday morning.

Reid: What do you want to do today, Stephanie?

Stephanie: Let's go down to the empty lot on the corner.

Reid: We were just there last weekend.

Stephanie: Well, we don't have anything else to do. Maybe we can start on the treehouse we've been planning.

Reid: Okay. I'll race you! Go!

Narrator: The twins reach the corner lot in a flash.

Reid: That's odd . . . do you hear something?

Stephanie: Yes, but where is it coming from?

Reid: It sounds like a kitten.

Stephanie: Look up! It is a kitten—up there in the tree. I'll climb up and get it.

Reid: What a cute kitten. It's all black and yellow with little white feet. Do you think Mom will let us keep it?

Stephanie: Let's go ask her.

(back at the house)

Reid: Mom, Mom! Look what we found! Isn't it cute?

Mom: What a darling little kitten.

Dad: Where did you find it?

Reid: In the empty lot on the corner.

Dad: Someone probably dumped it there. I think you might want to give it some milk.

Mom: You'd better run down to the pet store and buy some food. I'm sure that little tiger is hungry.

Narrator: In no time, Reid and Stephanie had run the two blocks to the small pet store.

Mr. Khan: Hello, kids. How can I help you today?

Reid: We just got a new kitten. We need some food.

Mr. Khan: I have special food just for kittens.

Stephanie: I think we'll need a lot, please.

Narrator: As Stephanie and Reid carry the cat food home, they realize the new kitten needs a name.

Reid: I've always wanted a kitten. What will we name it?

Stephanie: I like what Mom called it: Tiger.

Reid: Me, too. Then its name is Tiger.

Narrator: Back at home, the twins share their news.

Stephanie: We decided to name the kitty Tiger.

Mom: Well, it looks like we have a new member in our family. I've always wanted a kitten, too. They're so much fun!

Narrator: A week goes by . . .

Dad: You kids sure are spending a lot of time with Tiger. She's lots of fun. I love to watch her jump over the grass.

Reid: I like when she sleeps in bed with me. She's so warm. Her purring puts me to sleep.

Stephanie: I wish we could each have a kitty to sleep with.

Dad: Say, kids, I see we're almost out of kitten food. How about running down to the pet store to get some more?

Narrator: When the children get to the pet store . . .

Mr. Khan: So, you're back already. Your little kitten is a big eater. How many cans do you want this time?

Reid: I think we can each carry about 10 cans. Could you please put them in two bags?

Mr. Khan: Say, there were a couple of kids in here yesterday looking for their lost kitten.

Stephanie: Did they say what it looked like?

Mr. Khan: It was black and yellow, sort of spotty they said. Kittens get lost pretty easily. Keep an eye on that kitten of yours. You don't want it to get lost, too.

Narrator: As the children head home, Reid says aloud what each of them is thinking.

Reid: Stephanie, do you think Tiger is the lost kitten?

Stephanie: I don't know . . . What do you think we should do?

Reid: I don't know. I love Tiger. I don't want to give up Tiger.

Stephanie: Neither do I.

Reid: I sure would miss Tiger. I'll bet those kids miss their kitten, too. Maybe we should go talk to them and see if Tiger is their lost kitten.

Stephanie: I don't really want to, but I guess you're right.

Narrator: Stephanie and Reid walk back to the pet store, where Mr. Khan gives them the name and address of the children who lost their kitten. Since it's right in the neighborhood, the twins decide to walk to their house.

Stephanie: Wow, their house is close to the empty lot where we found Tiger.

Reid: It sure is!

Stephanie: Maybe we should just go on home.

Reid: But that's not right. You know that if we had lost Tiger, we would want her back.

Narrator: Stephanie and Reid knock on the door. A boy about their age opens it. His older sister soon joins him.

Uriel: Hello. Can I help you?

Stephanie: We heard you had lost a kitten.

Reid: We found a kitten in the empty lot, and we think it might be yours.

Nicole: What does the kitten look like?

Stephanie: She's black and yellow, with little white feet.

Uriel: That sure sounds like our kitten.

Reid: Maybe you'd like to come over and take a look.

Narrator: As soon as Nicole and Uriel get permission, the four children head to the twins' home to see the kitten.

Nicole: Patches! Oh, I'm so happy to see you!

Uriel: We didn't think we'd ever see you again!

Narrator: Reid and Stephanie are heartbroken to see the kitten go, but they know it is only right to return the kitten to her owners. Later that afternoon, the doorbell rings. Stephanie opens the door to find Nicole and Uriel standing there with two kittens in a box.

Stephanie: What's going on? Where did these kittens come from?

Uriel: We felt terrible about taking Patches away from you!

Nicole: But we knew the family with the mother cat still had two more kittens to give away. We thought you might like to have them.

Stephanie: Reid! You've got to come here right now!

Reid: This is awesome! Stephanie, I guess we can each sleep with a purring kitten from now on!

Uriel: Boy, there's nothing like a happy ending!

Name _____

The Lost Kitten

Draw a line from the beginning part of the sentence to the ending.
Be sure your sentences make sense.

1. Stephanie — was black and yellow with white feet.

2. The kitten — went to the pet store to buy kitten food.

3. The pet-store owner — told Stephanie and Reid the kitten was his.

4. "Patches" — wanted to go to the empty lot.

5. Stephanie and Reid — asked the kids to go buy more cat food.

6. Uriel — was the first to call the kitten "Tiger."

7. Mom — told Stephanie and Reid about the lost kitten.

8. Dad — was the name Uriel and Nicole gave their kitten.

Name _____

A Pet of My Own

Imagine you went to an empty lot on a corner. You heard a noise. Then you found an animal to take home for a pet. Draw a picture of the animal you would like to find. Then write about your pet.

[drawing box]

_____

_____

_____

_____

_____

Now Presenting...

Our Solar System

Journey through our solar system and learn facts about the planets that spin around our closest star, the Sun.

Setting the Stage

Background

Our solar system consists of a sun, nine planets, and various chunks of ice and rock known as asteroids, meteoroids, and comets. Each of these bodies is different and studied constantly by scientists on Earth.

Staging

Buy or make a drawing of each planet. Have the readers hold up the drawing of their planet when they read their lines.

Encore

To help students understand how we learn about space, check out the live feed from the Hubble Space Telescope on the NASA Quest Web site for children (http://quest.arc.nasa.gov/hst/).

Vocabulary

Introduce and discuss the following words before reading the script:

atmosphere: the air that surrounds Earth

extend: to stretch out

galaxy: a group of billions of stars that are part of a system

gravity: a natural force that makes things move toward the center of Earth

orbit: the path traveled by any heavenly body around another

tilt: tip

universe: everything that there is

vast: huge; enormous

Now Presenting...

Our Solar System

Our solar system consists of nine planets, a bright star, comets, meteorites, and asteroids. Each of these heavenly bodies is unique.

Characters

The Galaxy .... _____

The Solar System .... _____

The Sun .... _____

Mercury .... _____

Venus .... _____

Earth .... _____

Mars .... _____

Jupiter .... _____

Saturn .... _____

Uranus .... _____

Neptune .... _____

Pluto .... _____

Shooting Stars .... _____

_____

Our Solar System

······················· **Characters** ·······················

The Galaxy   Jupiter
The Solar System   Saturn
The Sun   Uranus
Mercury   Neptune
Venus   Pluto
Earth   Shooting Stars
Mars

The Galaxy: As you look at the sky, as you stare into space,
you might wonder where we fit into this place.
The universe is so large, our planet so small.
Where do we fit? Just where do we fall?

We're part of a galaxy called the Milky Way.
It's made of billions of stars, or so they say.
It's a cloud of stars you can see in the sky
if the night is clear and you have a sharp eye.

The Solar System: Nine different planets and one bright star
make up our solar system, which extends so far.
Some planets have moons, and some have rings.
Around our bright Sun they all do swing.
In orbits of varying sizes they race.
Nine planets and a sun go whirling through space.
Five planets of rock and four made of gas—
this is our solar system, and it's enormously vast.

The Sun: Way up in our sky is a large yellow ball.
It's gravity holds us so we don't fall.
It's really a star, but we call it the Sun.
It brings heat and light to everyone.
It's made up of gases that gravity holds.
It's over four and a half billion years old.

Mercury: Mercury, the first planet, is nearest the Sun.
It has little atmosphere. Moons? It has none!
With craters all over, it's a bare, rocky ball.
It's larger than Pluto, but still very small.
It's named after Mercury, a god from old Rome.
This planet's so hot it could not be our home.

Venus: Venus is named for a goddess of love.
It comes after Mercury in the heavens above.
Its size is like Earth's, with no moon in its sky.
While a day passes on Venus, an Earth year goes by.
Windstorms rage on Venus, and lightning flashes.
Its atmosphere is full of poisonous gases.

Earth: Earth, the watery planet, is third from the Sun.
It has a moon, but only just one!
It's surrounded by air for all living things.
The Earth is so special for the life it brings.
It's the fifth largest planet, and it isn't quite round.
The poles are a little bit flattened, we've found.

Mars: Mars is fourth from the Sun, a rust-colored ball.
With lots of volcanoes, Mars has the biggest of all:
the volcano Olympus Mons is three times as high
as Earth's Mount Everest, which is five miles high!
Two moons orbit Mars, which is half the Earth's size.
Are there Martians on Mars? No, those are just lies.

Jupiter: Jupiter is the biggest planet we know.
It's fifth from the Sun, with 17 moons that show.
Galileo, the astronomer, found the first four.
Since his time, we've spotted 13 moons more.
Jupiter's covered with clouds, and has a great red spot,
which we think is a storm on that planet so hot.

Saturn: With seven rings 'round it, Saturn's sixth in the line.
The rings, made of ice and rock, glimmer and shine.
Ten times larger than Earth, Saturn's second in size.
At least 30 moons orbit 'round in its skies.
Made mostly of gas, Saturn's considered quite light.
It could float in an ocean. Wouldn't that be a sight?

Uranus: Uranus is seventh, and it's tilted—that's true.
It's covered with gases; its color is blue.
Its moons circle 'round it—there's 20 we've found.
Its 11 rings spin, made of dust, dirt, and ground.
Did it crash with a planet a long time ago?
Is that why it's tilted? Scientists think so.

Neptune: Neptune is named for the god of the sea.
It's eighth in the lineup, with rings—one, two, three.
Neptune has eight moons; its color is blue.
It's made of gas, rock, and iron—and that's really true.
One hundred and sixty-four Earth years it takes,
for the very long trip 'round the Sun that it makes.

Pluto: Pluto is all the way out at the end.
A celestial snowball they call it, my friend.
It's ninth from the Sun and the smallest of all.
It's one-fifth Earth's size, and that's really small!
Charon is the name of its moon *(there's just one)*.
Pluto's four billion miles away from the Sun.

Shooting Stars: Asteroids, meteoroids, and comets, too,
circle our Sun and pass by our view.
Crashing and bumping, asteroids break into bits.
They become meteoroids, and they make quite a hit!
Some crash into planets, some fly through the sky.
They're called shooting stars.
Have you seen them go by?

All: Nine different planets and one bright star
make up our solar system, which extends so far.
Some planets have moons, and some have rings.
Around our bright Sun they all do swing.
In orbits of varying sizes they race.
Nine planets and a sun go whirling through space.

Name _____

Solar System Facts

Read the sentences below. Use the information to help you label each part of the diagram on page 141.

Sun: The Sun is a medium-size star at the center of our solar system.

Mercury: This planet is closest to the Sun.

Venus: The planet second from the Sun is about the same size as Earth.

Earth: The third planet from the Sun is mostly covered with water.

Mars: This red planet is fourth from the Sun.

Jupiter: The largest planet is fifth from the Sun.

Saturn: With six rings, this planet is sixth from the Sun.

Uranus: The seventh planet from the Sun has 11 rings.

Neptune: The eighth planet from the Sun is named after the Roman god of the sea.

Pluto: The farthest planet from the Sun is also the smallest planet.

Name _____

Our Solar System

Use the words in the box below to label this diagram in order, starting with the Sun.

~~Sun~~	Mars	Venus	Uranus
Earth	Neptune	Jupiter	Pluto
Asteroids	Mercury	Saturn	

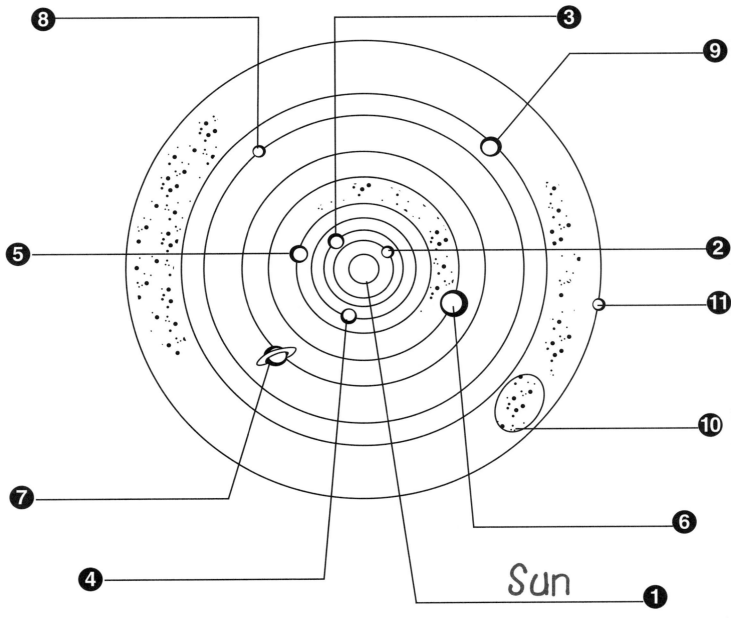

Sun

Our Solar System

Answer the following questions in complete sentences.

1. How many moons does Venus have?

   _____

2. Why is Mars called "the red planet"?

   _____

   _____

3. Which planet has the great red spot?

   _____

4. Which planet is named after the god of the sea?

   _____

5. Which planet has the tallest volcano?

   _____

6. Which planet would you like to live on? Explain why.

   _____

   _____

   _____

   _____

     Readers' Theater, Grade 2 • EMC 3307

Answer Key

John Chapman

page 14: States colored in red should include Massachusetts, Pennsylvania, Ohio, Illinois, Indiana, and Kentucky.

page 15: Drawings will vary.

page 16: Across: 2) berries; 3) roots; 7) seedling; **Down:** 1) pie; 2) blossoms; 4) shoes; 5) apple; 6) pan

Crow's Potlatch

page 24: Answers will vary.

page 25: Accordion book pages should be in the correct sequence. Drawings will vary.

Earth's Seven Continents

page 33:

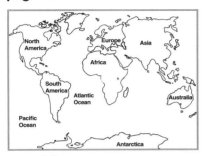

page 34:

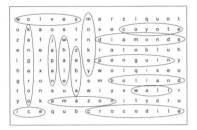

Febold Feboldson Saves Nebraska from Drought

page 41:

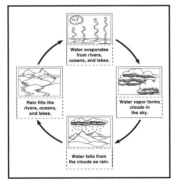

page 42: 1) T; 2) M; 3) T; 4) M; 5) T; 6) M; 7) T; 8) M; 9) T; 10) T

page 43:
1) the summer sky
2) ants
3) clover
4) night
5) honey
6) bee
7) pancake
8) ice
9) feather
10) thunder
11) Sentences will vary.
12) Sentences will vary.

The Statue of Liberty

page 50: Complete puzzle should depict picture of Statue of Liberty.

page 51: 1) France; 2) Mr. Bartholdi; 3) 1886; 4) seven; 5) July 4, 1776

page 52: 1) 18 minutes; 2) $13.00; 3) Answers will vary.; 4) 42 years old; 5) 429,200 pounds

The Foolish Little Hare: A Fable

page 60: Across: 3) coconuts; 6) cracking; 7) elephant; **Down:** 1) monkeys; 2) foolish; 4) tiger; 5) lion

page 61: Answers will vary.

Don't Forget Zero

page 68: 1) 7; 2) 12; 3) 365; 4) 24; 5) 20; 6) 100; 7) 3; 8) 80; 9) 20; 10) 12; 11) 20

page 69: 1) 100; 2) 60; 3) 75; 4) 800; 5) 47; 6) 147; 7) 305; 8) 79; 9) 760; 10) 90; 11) 490; 12) 1,000; 13) 968; 14) 68

page 70:

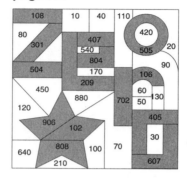

How Anansi Brought Stories to Earth

page 78: 1) stories; 2) a palm branch; 3) his wife; 4) his thread; 5) spider stories; Drawings will vary.

page 79: 1) 11 branches; 2) 13 feet deep; 3) 30 miles of thread; 4) 23 hornets; 5) 30 sticks

The Little Pollinators

page 87: 1) antenna; 2) eye; 3) head; 4) wing; 5) tongue; 6) pollen basket; 7) leg; 8) stinger

page 88:

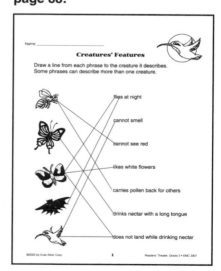

George Washington Carver

page 96: candy, dyes, flour, glue, ink, lotion, oil, paint, rubber, soap

page 97: From top right, clockwise: stem, peg, peanut, roots, soil level, yellow flower, leaf